SYKE

Sacrificed Your Kind Energy

RODNEY H. WASHINGTON

DEDICATION

I dedicate this book to the freedom of my cousin, Percy "Tommy" Johnson. Free. Percy "Tommy" Johnson, who's brilliant mind they could never incarcerate. Free. Percy "Tommy" Johnson, free of receiving a just appeal. Free. Percy "Tommy" Johnson, free of inadequate medical "care". Free. Percy "Tommy" Johnson, who's spirit is in a far greater place than 50 years behind the walls of that place. Free. I dedicate this book to my cousin, Percy "Tommy" Johnson, who is free.

ACKNOWLEDGEMENTS

Original Front Cover Art: Rodney H. Washington (Oil on canvas)

Back Cover Author Photo Credit: Tiffany DeVon (Photographic Eye)

*Pictured rocking select pieces:

Tiffany DeVon 1971 Jewelry Collection

*Herkimer Diamond Ring

*Herkimer Diamond Necklace

*Leather Fringe Necklace

Tiffany DeVon 1971 Haute Couture Collection

*Genuine Leather Fringe Vest w/ Rose Quartz

Hollywood Style Rocker Vibe One Of A Kind Hand Sculpted Works Of Art Herkimer Diamonds, Crystals, Genuine Stones/Leather (Discerning Eye)

A very special acknowledgement goes out to my lady, Tiffany DeVon, for offering "SYKE - Sacrificed Your Kind Energy" available for purchase on her Top Of The Line All-Natural Skincare Website: TiffanyDeVon1971.com

ABOUT THE AUTHOR

Bebop - Doo - Wop - Skippity - Skap - to the - Tippity - Tap - Tap - Tappin' - When I'm Typing - What I'm Writing - I-Do-It-How-Is-How-I-Do-It-How - Just like a jazz singer scattin',...(with my eyes closed!).

And so...

(Psst!)...(Hey, Reader!)...(JUST SO that YOU know!)...

I don't write to offend.
I write to offer.

For(You See)...

I write to push.
I DON'T write to appease!

And(Make NO Mistake!)...

I write as much to entertain,
AS MUCH AS I write TO teach!

For...

(I write to learn from what I'VE learned!)

And(In Turn!)...

):I write to heal and be healed:)

And(By ALL Means!)...

I write to be and remain in that creative "Zone"

FOR...

(I remain in pursuit of same with much zeal!)

And...

(PSST!)...(HEY, WORLD!!)...(PLEASE Let It Be Known!!!)...

I write by the style of "RODISM"

(An unusually-original-writing-style of my own!)

THOUGH...

I MUST say so,
It is a bit flattering,
Seeing thee adoption of "RODISM",
Across the different time zones!,

For(YOU SEE)...

By implementing paint strokes...

Of BIG BOLD LETTERS,
Author/Reader Interactions,

Italics & Dashes,
Marked Quotations,
With Double-Line-Spaces,
(And all those winks;) (And smiles:)
(That's ME giving YOU a wink;) ('Cause I made YOU smile:)
And lest WE forget,
The Unapologetic Fearless-Inflections,
WHICH ALL provides to thee aesthetics!,
(And MOST certainly!)...(Parentheses & Dots of 3),
('Cause that's ME arousing YOUR)...(Intrigue;)
FOR(YOU SEE)...
"RODISM" is Painting A Portrait Of Literacy!,

AND SO...
(Now that YOU ARE in the know!)...

YOU WILL begin to SEE what I SEE!!

And(That BEING!!)...

"RODISM" popping-up in everything,
From posts to memes,
EVEN periodicals,...(periodically;)

ALTHOUGH...

(Make NO Mistake!)...

I don't write for "inclusion",
Of the dually addictive and ridiculous -
Modern-Day-Popularity-Contest - fusion,
Being "played out" in real time,
Induced and welded to the carpal tunnel of the masses,
Fiending for that false affection,
By way, Of: This newfangled-form of "communication",

By way, Of: Thee abhorred harbored down in the keyboards,
By way, Of: Damages readily absorbed to be stored,
And, as such, into the mind,
By way, Of: One “Like”, “Follow”, “Share”, “Comment”, at a time!

For(YOU SEE!!!)…

I write, as I aspire,
For inclusion as a poet,
And that of a writer,
In the conversations,
That shall take place,
200 years from this date,
As one of the greatest ever,
To put ink on paper.

PREFACE

This book is a collect of poems I have written over the years. I remember as a little boy my father having a framed poem hanging in his den, of autumn being his favorite season that he penned. I wish I had that poem. Or at the very least, remembered exactly how it went. But I can tell you this much, that frame and glass pane could not contain the feel and smell of autumn. I am certain that I get my artistic and poetic abilities from my Dad.

I loved my childhood.

When my brother Norm and I were little boys, once a week, my Dad would have "Art Night" with us. It was all very fun and cool. We would draw, or make collages, or make volcanos out of paper mache and, once dried, we would paint them to look like real volcanos. (And as if that wasn't already fun and cool enough!) AND WHEN our Dad placed baking soda and vinegar into the mouths of the volcanos, it poured out like lava!

Fast forward to 1995 when my Dad died...

I morned my Dad for ten years straight.

Fast forward into and through...

As we add Bi-Polar into the equation. And then add on a not-so-healthy dose of decades of deep, deep, deep, deep, deep, depression. Add self-medication into the mix. Add in my multiple stays in the mental institutions. Add in my stay at rehab. Add in stress. And then post Traumatic in front of that. Add in horrible, horrible judgement. And tack-on my love affair with suicide. I was a complete fucking mess. But what helped me get through those times of all things,...was poety.

Some of the deepest, disturbing, angry, most-fucked-up disturbing poems (did I mention "disturbing" twice? Yes. YES I DID!! Let us move on)... you would ever (OR NOT!!!) want to read, was written by me during those days, nights, and years. (Poems with titles, such as: "Not-So Virgin Mary" & "Hot Cold Dead Girl")...(Did I mention the poems were angry and disturbed??)...(Let us move on)...

Fortunately enough (OR NOT!!), several years ago, I put approximately 300+ poems from those time periods in a dumpster. Some remained. Some I remembered. But most are gone for good.

What you are going to read in this book, are poems mostly written within the past 10-15 years or so. Within this book there's a wide spectrum, within that spectrum there's a menagerie, within the menagerie there's the minutiae, within the minutiae help and wisdom lies latent. I'm releasing this book upon the world to offer YOU the opportunity to read, heed, or waste it.

A good number of the poems in this book carry some of that deep, deep, deep, deep, deep depression mind-set, (NOT my current mind-set)... (by the grace of God!), BUT, DO contain a lot of that flavor! And why?

Because,...why the fuck not! Because,...my book, THIS BOOK, wouldn't be the same IF I DIDN'T put in there ALL the shit that, most people wouldn't have the guts to say aloud. BECAUSE,...TO NOT include it, and, TO NOT write it EXACTLY how I WOULD WRITE IT, would be of me, to capitulate. And I don't do that.

Even the best of people have been through the worst of times. People with degrees of higher education, 401k's, and home owners, are NOT my generalization of "best". (HOWEVER, by all means, they most certainly COULD be!). ALTHOUGH, by best, I'm talking about being NOT a hypocrite! By best, I'm talking about BEING a "seeker and speaker of truth"! By best, I'm talking about the one to give to the one, to provide aid to the one, to LISTEN to the one, the "one", that doesn't have much more than politeness, the "one", in dire need of kindness. Yes. THAT "best"! And yes. THAT "one"! For, you see, even the best of people have been through the worst of times. (Judge NOT, ya dig!) For, you see, take it from me, it's a short-quick-fuckin'-trip from "best" to "one"!

To me, the best stand-up comediennes and comedians throughout history, are the ones that have all been through some heavy shit. To me, the respect that I have for those fearless and unapologetic comediennes and comedians, comes from the fact that they all had the guts to bear the pain in their soul, and speak the truth in their heart, doing it their way. And, doing so in a way, to entertain, to teach, and to heal. And not necessarily in that order.

Poetry is my therapy. Writing is my therapy. Here's a collection of my therapy.

STATEMENT

"I've found, that, when the first line of a poem just comes to me, and, I just run with it from there, not knowing what the poem is going to be about, or, even what the next line of the poem is going to be, make for the best poems."

- RHW

CONTENTS

TRAVELS

TRAFFIC DANCE

And so...

Out his lungs he begins to blow,
The last of his hash of mustard green smoke,
Situated on his sofa he so sank,
Staying stuck on his sofa staring at his fish tank,

'Cause for whatever reason,...

FISH HAVE NEVER BEEN SO INTERESTING!!!,...

From that fish tank,
He would not glance,

The fish in the tank,
Put him in a trance,
Watching the fish,
Do the traffic dance!,...

A big truck comes up an on-ramp,
Moving, pushing, forcing,
The car in the right lane,
Over into the left lane,

But there's a car in the left lane,
Been in the left lane!,
And that car in the left lane,
Speeds up!,

That car that's been in the left lane,
Speeds up,
When the big truck,

Coming up the on-ramp,
Is coming up the on-ramp,

‘Cause the driver of the car,
That’s been in the left lane,
Is a prick,

And besides,
It’s human nature,

And...

THAT driver knows the traffic dance!,

The dance of traffic. The on-ramp shuffle.

Big truck comes up on-ramp,
Car in right lane moves to left lane,
Car in left lane speeds up,

‘Cause the driver of the car,
Speeding up,
In the left lane,
Is a prick,

And besides,
It’s human nature,

And that’s the dance of traffic!

The traffic dance. The on-ramp shuffle.

And though,
The dance has commenced,
Not all have yet,
Begun to dance,
The dance of traffic,

The traffic dance. The on-ramp shuffle.

Those on the wall,
Not yet dancing,
The wall of traffic,
All have seen,
That those three,...

The-big-on-ramp-truck,
The-right-lane-to-left-lane-car,
And the-prick-
that's-been-in-the-left-lane -
And now speeding up,...

Have all broken the ice,
And have begun to dance,
The dance of traffic,

The traffic dance. The on-ramp shuffle.

And so,
They all grab a dance partner!,
And exit the wall,
And enter the dance floor,
Gettin' down with the dance of traffic!,

The traffic dance. The on-ramp shuffle.

Now off the wall,
And they're all,
Speeding up,
And maneuvering,
To avoid,
Or stay ahead of,

Stay in front of,
Don't want to be behind of,...

The big truck,
The-right-lane-to-left-lane-car,
Who's also speeding up,
And maneuvering for,
The big truck,
And speeding up,
And maneuvering for,
The car that's been in the left lane,
Who's been speeding up,
'Cause that driver's a prick,

And besides,
It's human nature,

The dance of traffic. The traffic dance. The on-ramp shuffle.

The car that's been in the left lane,
And been speeding up,
Doesn't want,
The-big-on-ramp-truck -
Or the-right-lane-to-left-lane-car,
To be in front,
To get ahead,
And what's worst,
To be first,
'Cause the-car-that's-been-in-the-left-lane-
and-been-speeding-up -
driver's a prick,

And besides,
It's human nature,

And onward goes the dance of traffic...

The traffic dance. The on-ramp shuffle.

The left lane car,
That's been in the left lane,
Speeds up,
The big on-ramp truck,
Moves from the on-ramp,
To the right lane,
THEN ONCE in the right lane,...
THE BIG TRUCK SPEEDS UP!!!,

'Cause the driver of the big truck,
Doesn't want,
The car that's maneuvered from,
The right lane to the left lane,
Being pushed over,
By the big truck,
Avoiding the big truck,
So that the big truck,
Can maneuver from,
The on-ramp to the right lane,
To get in front,
To be in front,
And what's worst,
To be first,

Which would drive,
The big-truck-driver insane,
For it to be in front of it,
In the right lane!,

'Cause the-driver-of-

the-big-truck -
Is a prick,

And besides,
It's human nature,

So the-right-lane-to-the-left-lane-car,
Then speeds up,
And goes back to the right lane,
Getting in front,
Of the big truck,
That was on the on-ramp,
But that's now in the right lane,...

'Cause the driver of -
the-right-lane-to-left-lane-back-to-right-lane-car,
Doesn't want,
The big on-ramp truck,
That's now in the right lane,
To be in front,
To be ahead,
And what's worst,
To be first,

'Cause the-driver-of-
the-right-lane-to-left-lane-to-right-lane-car,
Is a prick,

And besides,
It's human nature,

The dance of traffic. The traffic dance. The on-ramp shuffle.

The-car-that's-been-in-the-left-lane-
that's-been-speeding-up,

Stays in the left lane,
And stays speeding up!,...

Staying ahead of both,
The big truck that was,
On the on-ramp,
But now in the right lane,
AND the-right-lane-
to-left-lane-
back-to-right-lane-car,

'Cause the driver of the car,
That's been in the left lane,
And that's been speeding up,
Doesn't want,
The big on-ramp truck,
That's now in the right lane,
Or the-right-lane-
to-left-lane-
back-to-right-lane-car,
To get ahead,
To be in front,
And what's worst,
To be first!,
'Cause the driver's a prick,

AND besides,
It's human nature!,

The dance of traffic. The traffic dance. The on-ramp shuffle.

And up ahead,
You just know that,
There's a speed trap,

Up ahead!,

Hiding. Hidden. Harboring.

But the driver of the car,
Speeding in the left lane,
That's been in the left lane,
Isn't thinking,
About the possibility,
Of something hiding,
A speed trap possibly,
Up ahead,
Simply,
NOT thinking ahead!,

Hiding. Hidden. Harboring.

'Cause the-been-in-the-left-lane-
been-speeding-up-driver,
Just can't be behind,
Just gotta be ahead,
Just gotta go fast,
Just can't be last,
And what's worst,
Just gotta be first!,
'Cause that driver's a prick,

And besides,
It's human nature,

AND...

YOU KNOW,
There's just GOTTA' always be,
That one on the dance floor,...

You know,
There's just always gotta be,
THAT ONE DRIVER for sure!,...

There's ALWAYS one,
PAINFULLY-OBLIVIOUS to the fact,
THAT,...the traffic dance has commenced!,

AND...

Just says, *"Fuck it!"*,

And doesn't move,
The fuck over,
Or speed,
The fuck up!,

Fucking up,
The traffic dance!,

AS...

The dance of traffic,
Gets ALL fucked up!!!,

The dance of traffic. The traffic dance. The on-ramp shuffle.

And that's what he sees,
As he sits there,
Stuck.

On that sofa,
Staring into that fish tank,
Stuck!

As...

The-by-far-largest -
Of three catfish,
In the tank waters,
From one side,
To the other,

Back-and-forth,
Back-and-forth,
Back-and-forth,
In a perpetual swim,

Over,
And over,
And over,
Again,
Pushing the-two-
far-smaller of the three -
Catfish to the opposite,
Tank side,
A rather,
I'd rather,
Drown,
In this tank,
Life,
In avoidance,
Of the-far-largest -
Of the three catfish,
Maneuvering,
To get away,
And stay away,
From the-far-largest -
Of the three catfish,
In perpetual avoidance,...

And in this fish tank,
There ain't no wallflowers,
For the-far-more-largest -
Of the three catfish,
Won't allow it!,

For as far as,
The-far-largest -
Of the three catfish,
As it does this,
Back-and-forth,
Back-and-forth,
Back-and-forth,
In the tank waters,
From one side,
To the other,
In a perpetual swim,
Over,
And over,
And over,
Again,...

There's a multitude,
Of some kind of species,
For safety,
In a group,
Of even-smaller-fish,
They all swim,
To the opposite,
As the-far-largest -
Of the three catfish,
While in avoidance,
Of the-far-largest -

Of the three catfish,
WHILE STILL HAVING TO,
Well at least,
They're TRYING to,
Avoid and maneuver,
While staying in a group,
Around and away,
From the-far-smaller-catfish,
Yeah,...
THOSE OTHER TWO!!,

Back-and-forth,
Back-and-forth,
Back-and-forth,
In the tank waters,
From one side,
To the other,
In a perpetual swim,
Over,
And over,
And over,
Again,...

Those multitude,
Of smaller-fish,
Of some kind of species,
Swim for safety,
AND FOR safety,
Swim in a group,
They DON'T have an easy life!,
And yet,
ALL THE WHILE,
A BIG funky-looking-fish,

That could PROBABLY,
Fuck-up quite EASILY,
The-far-largest -
OF the three catfish,
Remains,
And just stays,...

Hidden. Harboring. Holed up.

In a rock cave!,
Down amongst,
The sediment,
The fish dookie,
And the gunk!,

While,
AND ALL THE WHILE,
A gigantic-algae-eater-fish,
Just says,
"Fuck it!",
Staying on the glass,
In one spot,
STUCK!

Back-and-forth,
Back-and-forth,
Back-and-forth,
In the tank waters,
From one side,
To the other,
In a perpetual swim,
Over,
And over,

And over,
Again,
The-far-largest -
Of the three catfish,
Moves the fish along,
'Cause the-far-largest -
Of the three catfish,
Is a prick!

And besides,
It's only nature!

That's some *good* ass *hash,* huh?

THE SOUNDS OF MORNING

The career choices made,
The families one was born into,
Of those playing the game,
And making all the right moves and decisions,
Proceeds,

Proceeding all across America,
The sounds of the morning,
Are taking place,

(What's that sound?)

The sound any working man would know,
The sound any roommate, wife, child,
Or significant other,
Of a working man would know,

(What's THAT sound???)

The sound of a razor,
Being banged against,
The upper area,
Of a bathroom sink bowl,
To rinse,
Just to the right,
(OR left!),
Of that tiny - this-is-to-prevent-
the-sink-from-overflowing - drain,
As razors get banged,

After several passes,
Several times,

Several times over,
For several more passes,
According to the amount of -
Shave-By-Numbers-Real-Estate -
On the necks and faces,
In accordance to the shave,

And then banged,
Repeatedly, again,
Against the upper area,
All across America,
Shaven-whisker displacement,
Off the necks and faces,

And from faces and necks,
As razors get banged,
Repeatedly, the same,
By the tiny drain,
Just to the right,
(OR left!),
(As the case may be!),

Knocking free,
Fresh-cut-stubble-and-whiskers,
From all the ridiculous,
Amounts of blades,
In between,
The-freshly-cut get stuck -
Impacted and sandwiched -
And packed in place,
In between,
A union is made,
Stubble and whiskers,

Add texture to the mixture!,
Mixed-up-in-with all of those,
Fresh-nicks-mixed-with shaving cream,
Have become a bloody-foam!,

The cadence of it all,
The running waters,
The splashing of the waters,
In the bowls of sinks,

Of the rinsing,
And of the banging free,
Of the mortar-like hardened
pink-tinged cream,

And of the stubbles,
Mud, grasses and twigs,
Cautionary log cabin-esk sidings,

Which requires,
More intensified banging,
Providing,

More intensified ample-audibles,
Through closed bathroom doors,
If one so-gives-a-fuck,
Or has the time,

Of thc banging of thc razors,
All across America,
Of the sounds of morning,

Of the sounds of morning,
All across America,
Of the banging on the bathroom doors,

Of the, “MOM, SHE’S STILL IN THE BATHROOM!!!”,
Of the, “MOM, SHE USED UP ALL THE HOT WATER!!!”,
Of the, “YOU’RE GONNA’ BE LATE FOR THE SCHOOL BUS!!!”,

Of the, “IF YOU MISS THE BUS,
I’M NOT DRIVIN’ YOU TO SCHOOL!!!,

Of the, “YOU’LL BE WALKIN’!!!
AND DON’T LET ME GET A CALL,
AT MY NEW JOB,
THAT YOU WERE LATE!!!”,

Of the, “I told you, you were going to be crying in the morning!,
Tonight, you’re going to bed at seven!”

Of hot water,
Being poured into hot cereal,
Of the spoons in bowls,
Stirrin’ it up!,

All across America,
Of the sounds of morning,
Of the sounds of morning,
All across America,

Of the unmistakable-feeling of the sound,
(to some),
Of two pieces of styrofoam,
Being pressed and rubbed together,

Of the sound,
Of hardened-lifetime-brake-pads,
Being pressed and rubbing against -
blued - from-heat-and-wear - rotors,

All across America,

Of the morning rush,
Of turnstiles and of tokens,
Of the sounds of morning,
Of the sounds of morning,
All across America,
Of commentaries made,

Of, "That guy has a loose serpentine belt.",
Of, "That asshole shouldn't be in the carpool lane!,
Where's a cop when you need one!?",

Of commuters bitching about,
The car in front of them,
Not having their money ready,
At the toll booth!,

Of commuters threatening,
And letting it be known,
"Get out of my way!,
And you best not make me,
miss this subway!",

Of the approach,...

Of the, "Oh damn!,
This muthafucka' is gonna,
sit next to me again!",
Of the, "Move your ass over,
you're sittin' too close!",

Of the sounds of morning,
All across America,
The sounds of morning,
Are taking place.

ORANGE JULIUS

As he walks he believes,
From what he feels,
From what he sees,
That he has his bearings,
Goin' as the wind blows,
Ain't runnin' no errands,
In his travels,
He knows where he's at,
But that would be until he walks past,
The huge parking lot of the City Mall,
As the result,
Of bearing witness to,
The noisy-public-nuisance,
Created by the cup from Orange Julius,
And the Auntie Anne's pretzel,
Someone lazy,
Placed into it!,
As a result,
The litter-strewn parking lot,
Is where - life vs life - gets fought and lost,
by a large group of SEAGULLS!!!,
            OF WHICH - GOT him -
                EXACTLY - WHERE-THE-FUCK-HE'S-AT -
            NOW - TRYING TO RECALL!!!,...
"Damn!,
I thought I was more "inland",
than I am!,
I swear I woulda' swore!,

BUT...
after seeing all these seagulls??,
Hmm,...
I MUST BE DOWN THE SHORE!!!".

BASKETBALL COURTS

And so...

His mind,
It rages!!!,

As...

His travels takes him past,
Basketball courts enclosed by cages,

Sending the neighborhood kids the subliminal message,
This is your ONLY way out!,

You can break free of the neighborhoods,
If you can break through the chains,

So...

Even those,
Flying high or drunk,...

Try to break the chain nets off the rims,
With tomahawk dunks,

Sneaky and deceptive by the city,
And you don't even know it,

Same reason why...

The courts are still littered,
With baggies and cracked pipes,

The youth play in vacant grass lots,
Windblown with plastic shopping bags,
On which that,

The shop owners on won't be taxed,
For seven years,

The youths that aren't playing games in the lots,
Are on the courts learning how to dunk,
Or learning to play the game,
That can net them seven years,

The sights in this city,
Like the homeless blindman in the middle of the street,
Dismissed by cop cars or not,
Are enough to bring him to tears.

SASSAFRAS ROOTS

And...

Just up ahead,
There's a pimp standing up ahead,
With a pair,
Of pimpin'-ass gator skin cowboy boots,
Hangin' from a wire,
Over his head,

And...

The pimp's ONLY overhead,
Is his bottom bitch, "BIG HUSKY"!,

And...

(She's a down-ass bitch!)...

Tha' type-a-bitch,
To place a fresh cigarette,
Up to a pimp's lips!,

Tha' type-a-bitch,
To then,
Light-up that bitch,
Fo' a pimp!,

Tha' type-a-bitch,
To do THAT shit,
ALL night,
Fo' HER pimp!,

Tha' type-a-bitch,
A pimp,

AIN'T EVEN GOTTA' snap his fingers,
AT a bitch,
Fo' her,
TO DO that shit!,

Tha' type-a-bitch,
Wit big ol' breasts!!,
(proceeded by!!),
Her big ol' nipples,
(I MUST confess!!),
Just JUTTIN' through,
Her skintight dress!!,

Tha' type-a-bitch,
That'll make a trick,
Peep ALL the angles!,
(WHILE HE'S TRYNA'-fig'a-out -
WHICH body part of BIG HUSKY'S -
Is lookin' THE MOST PAINFUL!!!),...

Be it...

Her: Ten "sausage-links" -
Strapped-down -
In them open toes!,

OR,(be it!)...

The: "SECTIONAL-BULGING",
(from her knees down to her ankles!),...

CAUSED BY...

Her: knee-high-high-heel-stiletto-Roman-Gladiator-cross-laces,...
(CUTTIN' OFF her circulation!!!),

AND SO...

IT'S JUST them two!!,
'TIL mutha' fuckin' tricks come thru,...
(tryna' get lucky!),

'CAUSE...

"Tha' Game" GOT thrown off track!,
Oh, 'bout,...
A year or so back!,

AND SO, (AND, BUT NOW!)...

OUT ON "THA' TRACK",
IT JUST BE - "BIG HUSKY" - IN THIS TOWN!!!

And so...

THIS big thorough-ass "Bottom Bitch",
GONNA' hold it down!,

'CAUSE, (AS we, all know!)...

A pimp NEED HIS money!

AND...

THIS THOROUGH-ASS-THICK-GIRL,
She be goin' by the name of,...
"BIG HUSKY"!!!,

And...

The pimp,
Stays fly-as-fuck!,
Stays coolin',
Between a couple of puffs,

And(though)...

The pimp might fuck around,...
This-here pimp AIN'T NO -
MUTHA' FUCKIN' - CLOWN!,

And...

Fo' "THA' GAME" and,
Fo' THIS CITY,
A pimp,
TRYNA' hold it down!,

FOR...

THIS-HERE PIMP rocks,
Lion heads and BIG gold crosses,
Layin' heavy,
'Pon his three-piece-suits,

And...

They hangin' heavy,
From gold ropes,
Thick n' busy,
Like sassafras roots!!!,

Tha' type-a-pimp,
TO STAY,
Well-groomed,
(BUT NEVER a groom!),

Tha' type-a-pimp,
TO STAY,
TRYNA' catch himself a bitch!,
(Fill'er-up wit drinks!),

THEN...

"Seal tha' deal",
In the back,
Of the back,
Of a strip club's back,
Private lapdance room!,

Tha' type-a-pimp,
To LET you know,
HE LIVIN' RIGHT,
BY his fingernail length!,

FOR...

(Long "Pimp Hand" fingernails,
AIN'T FOR YOU SQUARES!),...

BUT...

IT WORK FO' A PIMP!

And...

Wit them - Pampered - Well-Manicured -
Clear-Finished-Nail-Polished - "Money-Counters" -
A pimp DON'T count HIS money,
'Til tha' night IS FINISHED!!!,

'CAUSE...

After a bitch,
Give A PIMP'S MONEY to a pimp?,

(A bitch'll BE empty-handed!)

SO...

"Get back-out-there bitch!",...

AND...

"DON'T BE comin' back EMPTY-HANDED!!",...

'CAUSE...

(THEM EMPTY-HANDS of a bitch?),...

Well...

(A bitch GOTS'TA' REPLENISH!!!),...

FOR...

HE'S tha' type-a-pimp,
THAT STAYS wit,
Ridiculous-diamond-blingers,
SITTIN' HIGH atop,
Of EACH ONE of his fingers!!!!!!!!!,

Tha' type-a-pimp,
THAT STAYS shaped-up wit,
Deep-rolling-waves,
Down to the root!,

Tha' type-a-pimp,
THAT STAYS FRESH from his,
Big-brim Bailey on down to HIS,
OWN genuine leather,
Tail-cut gator,
Skin shoes!,

Tha' type-a-pimp,
Fo' a lonely-hungry type-a-bitch,
A pimp,
STAY TRYNA' BE RECRUITIN'!,

And...

(HE DON'T don't pack no pistol!)

'CAUSE...

HE THA' TYPE-A-PIMP,
THAT GON' LET HIS,
MOUTH DO THA' SHOOTIN'!,

For...

HE'S tha' type-a-pimp,
THAT STAY shootin' his,
Mouth-off instead!,

AND...

THIS-HERE-PIMP,
Be goin' by the name of,...
"WEEKEND FRED"!!!

SELF-ENTITLED SENSATIVES

As his travels continues,
He bears witness to,
Too many,
Too emotionally-sensitive,
Too emotionally-draining,
Too-dismissive,
(to, and), OF: VALID points,
BEING (and) TOO bullheaded-upon,
OF: ONLY WHAT they WANT to do!!,

(OF WHICH)...

These too-damn sensitive,
(and) TOO-DAMN-DRAINING YOUTHS,
ARE NOT WILLING to do,
The Things: They GOT TO do FIRST,

(IN ORDER)...

TO GET to THAT POINT IN LIFE,
OF: NOW I can do,
WHAT I WANT to do!!!,

And(IMAGINE THIS!)...

FROM NOTHING MORE,
(AND NOTHING LESS!) THAN,
DUE TO: Puttin' in that HARD WORK first!!!!,

(((OY-HARDHEADED&LAZY-VEY!!!)))

Having in his sites,
TOO many "Self-Entitled-Sensitives",
Giving EVERY EXCUSE,

As to WHY,
They CAN'T work!,
WHILE PLACING BLAME UPON YOU,
AS TO WHY,
YOUR guidance and advice,
WON'T work!!,

(Yeah,...sadly:(...(THAT BULLSHIT!!!)

AS(WELL, AS)...

In his sites,
A world that's only getting worse,
With no getting any better in sight,
Peeping the city's fallacies,
The City's: FREE-of-Forming-Calluses,
(((ain't-got-none!!!))),
Lumberjacks-of-Man-Buns -
AND - The: Eyebrows-on-Fleek -
Employment-and-Common-Sense -
NEVER-Seek - COMMUNITIES!!!

((((((OY-TO-THA'-FUCKIN'-VEY!!!!!!))).

AND SO...

(He can't take it no mo'!)...

And(he)...

DIPS-THE-FUCK-OFF,
Of these even sidewalks,
CHOCK-FULL, OF:
"Self-Entitled-Playin'-Make-Believe-Masses!",

As(HE)...

Runs as fast as he can,
DOWN and THROUGH an embankment,
(steep and full),
Of: tall-and-all-
bent-over-dead-
December's-weeds-and-grasses!

HEART OF A LION, MIND OF A WOLF

Heart of a lion,
Mind of a wolf,
God and the Devil,
Were right there with me,
With each step that I took,

Heart of a Lion,
Mind of a Wolf,
The last step that I took,
Was the last step that I took,

Caught up in the whirlwind,
A Natural Born Loose Cannon,
Cocky as fuck when I'm pissed off,
That's why I were this shit eatin' grin,

The Devil's in that meth,
Sniff her up, or past the test?,
For my soul, she never rests,
So to that, I say God Bless,

I live my life like with each step,
It might be kill or be killed,
With the very next,

You never know when,
You'll be Blessed,
With the last step,
Of oh sweet Death,

Some people are just,
So damn blind,

That today they won't die,
In a fatal car crash,
Or from a violent crime,

They never think that today,
An aneurysm could blow your mind,
So I'm ready for Death,
With each step of mine,

Heart of a Lion,
And on some mental-Wolf-shit,
You want to kill me?,
You gonna HAVE TO work hard for it!,

Your eyes will get big,
When you get your throat slit,
With your blood on my boots,
Might make my next step stick!,

And even though I do bad,
God tested me with the choices I had,
When I die don't cry or be sad,
Ever see a smirk on a dead man's face like he's glad?,

Serpents and booze,
Are a man's ruin,
Keep your trust,
I don't want a new friend,

That's a good choice,
I'll just keep it pushin',
And from my bad choices,
I know the cop's are lookin'!,

Size 13's,

One step at a time,
And even though this life,
Hasn't always been kind,

I've lived the Hell out of this,
Life of mine,
Another like me,
I know you will never find,

There will never be,
Another like me,
I'm a one of a kind,
And that ain't hard to see,

You scared little sheep,
Of you the world has plenty,
Me conforming to your flock?,
That shit will never be,

Don't be scared,
Of a motherfucking thing,
Just be ready to kill or die,
With what the next step may bring,

When I die,
Will the Angels sing?,
When I die,
Will I be Blessed with Angel Wings?,

Would I change a thing,
Of my life of sinnin'?,
Not a chance in hell,
I'm tougher than,
Whatever you may be bringin'!,

Heart of a Lion,
Mind of a Wolf,
God and the Devil,
Were right there with me,
With each step that I took,

Heart of a Lion,
Mind of a Wolf,
And the last step that I took,
Was the last step that I took,

Heart of a Lion,
Mind of a Wolf,
God and the Devil,
Were right there with me,
With each step that I took.

MAMMOTH FACTORIES OF EXTINCTION (PRELUDE)

He drives past the rowhouses,
That are slammed together,
They ain't stuck together,
These bitches are slammed together!,

No front stoops,
Slammed together so tight,
Each front door nearly touches,
The neighboring neighbor's front door!,

Packed them in tight,
To house the neighborhood working poor,
In the mammoth neighborhood factories,
Where the neighbors don't even work there no more!,

Now...

Some get clowned-on,
For working on,
Their grades,

Others...

Get dissed,
For working on,
Learning a trade,

Workin' on...

Brainwashin' the ones trying.

That...

They are just wasting their time!

And...

The ones that were working,
In the factories,
Are working on,
Not losing their minds!

MAMMOTH FACTORIES OF EXTINCTION

He drives across the town at dusk,
Passing block after block of not much,

Rows and rows of rowhouses and store fronts,
With neon Life Insurance signs and such,

Every other corner has a bodega,
Yellow canvas awning crowned,

And completing the process,
Of inner city real estate hopscotch,

Corner bars allowingly land,
On the remaining staggered blocks,

There's plenty of traffic on the streets,
Taxis, buses, and trolleys run through the city,

A large gathering of you-best-be-from-around-here,
Battle to determine who's the best rapper from around here!,

Most shop owners are closing up shop for the day,
Rolling down their I-hope-this-is-enough-to-keep-from-getting-robbed-gates,

Mammoth factories long since extinct,
With windows punched out like timecards,

Perennially abide at will to the receipt of graffiti,
Like some plastic cemetery flowers,

The artistic displays both new and old,
By the people that return there,

Conjure remembrances of a once spirited place,

That the workers no longer provide,

While the factories' high barbed wire topped chain-link fences,
At the sidewalks' edge,

Remain engaged in the courtship of host or parasite,
With the committed trees they've grown attached to.

GOOD TIME MADE

Timing lights,
Making good time,
'Cause he's been peeping the city,
And the city's been peeping him,
Faces and cars change,
Like the changing lights,

He makes good time,
As he drives past,
The placement of the dialysis clinics,
Due to the over abundance,
Of fried foods and sugary substances,
That have been placed in the communities now,
For quite some time,

Driving past the place,
Where lifeline needles are placed,
In shunts in place,
For those placed in the chairs therein,
The next place for them,
Is a life of blindness,
The prosthetist's office and,
The grave,

Good time made,
As he travels past,
Those lined up at the rehabs,
And the methadone clinics,
They come-and-go out of the doors -
Like woven-lines-of-bullshit -
Out their mouths,...

"I need money,
for smokes and gas,
so I can make it to my appointment.",
(Sold the smokes,
And the Suboxone strips,
To get high,
From off that needle point),...

"Oh my God!,
I need more gas money!,
I start my new job in the morning!",
(Showed up for the two days -
Of paid training -
AND ain't been seen back at,
That new job since!),...

Ain't got no job,
BUT mission accomplished!,
Made just enough money -
To: "get back at it",
(Just to blowup loved ones phones again!),...
(How long before they're the ones in mourning?),...

Good time made,
Driving past the lines,
Lined up,
Sellin' blood at the blood banks,
(Donating pints and ounces,

To flip that shit,
For pints and ounces!!),
While weaving stories,
For the P.O.'s,
On how they are so afraid,

Of the needle,
(BUT bright and early in the morning,
The blood banks can stick it in!),

The hot-piss-lines,
Do find the ways,
So they can't piss for the P.O.'s,
(BUT can piss and moan all day,
That YOU haven't done enough for them!).

AUDIS AND ACURAS

Audis and Acuras,
Hyundais and Hondas,
Wherever I be,
That's where I find ya'!,

Fords are a bore,
Coupes love to snoop,
And lurking down the highways,
Are Subarus too,

A black Chevy Suburban?,
Awe c'mon, man!,
They stick out about as much,
As white Sprinter vans!,

WHEREVER I'm at?,
THAT'S WHERE THEY ARE!!!,
NEVER seen so many on cell phones,
Parked in their cars:)

And, uh,
We'll just call it fate,
'Cause, lookie-lookie here,
Here comes ANOTHER Municipal Plate!,

And they're ALL eyeballing me!,
Oh, how can this be??,
Like getting a new friend request,
That only has two friends,...maybe three;)

It's just soooooo damn clever!,
Y'all gonna HAVE TO do better!,

And I'ma let y'all know - I'm only getting high,
I ain't about no hand-to-hand cheddar,
(Hope y'all banking a lot of overtime!),
('Cause, to me - it's whatever;)

ALL I GOT, ALL I WANT

I got whiskey, a warrant, and a woman at home,
Kissed my baby on her cheek,
Said I don't know how long I'll be gone,
I'm on the run, but I ain't alone,
'Cause I got whiskey, a warrant, and a woman at home,

Some drunk tough guy in a black Cat Diesel Power cap,
Gave his woman a smack,
'Round here we don't play that,
I took his life, I took his truck, I took his cap, and his bottle of Jack,
Gotta make it to Juarez, while the sky's still black,

I got whiskey, a warrant, and a woman at home,
Kissed my baby on her cheek,
Said I don't know how long I'll be gone,
I'm on the run, but I ain't alone,
'Cause I got whiskey, a warrant, and a woman at home,

Made it back home and threw some clothes in a sack,
Dug up the mason jar full of cash buried out back,
Kissed my baby on her cheek,
Said I don't know how long but baby I'll be back,
Gotta make it to Juarez, while the sky's still black,

I got whiskey, a warrant, and a woman at home,
Kissed my baby on her cheek,
Said I don't know how long I'll be gone,
I'm on the run, but I'm not alone,
'Cause I got whiskey, a warrant, and a woman at home,

Highway patrol shot out all 18 wheels, and I shot back,
Brought me before the judge, with the charges stacked,

Said a 'hundred years hard time, I'm gonna break your back,
Told the judge, your bars will never hold me, told my baby I'd be back,

And don't you know...

I got whiskey, more warrants, and no woman at home,
Got my baby sittin' right up on me, and all we do is roam,
We on the run, but we ain't alone,
'Cause we got whiskey, more warrants, and the road is our home.

LONG GONE

No love of my life,
No friends or a wife,
And my daughter thinks I'm shit,
So I'ma take a lil' trip,

Nobody will know where I'm going,
Just me and this poem,
And I'm sorry Mom and Dad,
I must have been born sad,

Don't want to feel like this no more,
And plus life is a bore,
Can't trust no one no more,
Don't know much but I am sure,...

I won't be coming back,
And that's a fact jack!,
YOU can have the life I knew,
Don't want it, I am through,

And...

By the time you realize,
I'm gone,...
I'll be long gone.

PILGRIMAGE

I'm going out to Oakland,
And I'm never coming back,
I'm going out to the land,
Of the Silver and Black,
I'll cross the stateline,
Like I'm crossing the line of scrimmage,
Finally on my Mecca pilgrimage,
Once I arrive,
I'll never be so alive,
I'll get a job selling ice cream on the beaches,
Then I'll blow my brains to pieces,
After I wade out into the East Bay,
And I know I won't decay,
Rocks in my pockets to make sure I sink,
On my blood the fish will drink,
On my fluids seahorses will sip,
(And them lil' bastards best-slurp up all of it!),
On my meat the crabs will pick,
(And them lil' bastards best-not waste a bit!),
On the shore a little boy will point,
With that cone of his that runs and drips,
Ice cream off his elbow joint,
("Dad, look-here! Out in the Bay! Come quick!,
LET'S me and you take a selfie pic!,
With all those seagulls in the background goin' at it!"),
I want all y'all to remember this,
Be you with your lover or with your kids,
Bombarded by seagulls as they dive,
Relentlessly after your boardwalk fries,

Or feverishly fiending to be feasting on your funnel cake,
(On me, they did so grab a taste!),
Hot bird shit?,
That ain't it!,
THAT'LL be me shittin' on y'all,
In your hair runnin' down to your face,
IN the form of human waste!,
But before all that and me will be the East Bay,
(You know, before out into it I wade!),
To go and go do it,
As I get into it!,
Once in place on my liver I'll place,
The final dying wish off my Bucket List,
For an eagle to come swoop down,
And tear it out,
And dine on it!,
Yes indeed, I'll be dead for years,
Guess I always knew there would be no tears,
Yes indeed not one soul will know,
('Cause I ain't tellin' ANYBODY when I go!),
I'm going out to Oakland,
And I'm never coming back.

SYKE PARK

Back down the steps,
And then back in the car,
Back down the sidewalk,
The curb with the bar,
Back down the street,
With plenty on his mind,...

And(then)...

Back on his mother fuckin' fuck y'all grind!

Same ol' shit...

The homeless,
The addicts,
The cypher under a chocolate canopy,
Coughing like asthmatics,

Looking over,
As he passes SYKE Park,
Where what's done in the daytime,
Is done in the dark,
Lookin' like the LOVE Sculpture,
In the City of Brotherly Love,

But...

(At SYKE Park)...

YOU AIN'T finding NO love!

And...

YOU AIN'T finding NO hugs!

BUT...

(YOU CAN find PLENTY)...

Self-medicating THEIR heartache WITH drugs!!!

The SYKE Pedestal Sculpture,
So parked in SYKE Park,
Where the heartbroken park themselves,
AND self-medicate,
From morning 'til dark,

"SY" stacked on top of "KE",
"KE" stacked beneath "SY" on the bottom,
It's the sculpture for ALL lovers,
Who been done rotten!,

Big red-lettered SYKE,
Put up on display,
Placed on a pedestal,
For "so-called" love's decay,

With the big red letter "Y",
Leaning far to the right...tipping over,
Beautifully-flawed,
Up on that pedestal,...

FOR...

(THE MOST heartbroken question EVER ASKED,...that's regrettable!)...

"WHY didn't I see pedestals were reserved, for TRUE loves?"

NOW...

(The ones WHO GOT played??)...

Are in SYKE Park,...playing with drugs!

The SYKE Sculpture Pedestal,
Is made in BIG BOLD RED LETTERS,
Paying homage TO THE heartbroken,
ON TOP of a pedestal!,

"SY" stacked on top of "KE",
Painted heartbreak-red,
And placed on a TALL pedestal,
FORGED from the DISCARDED scraps,
OF cast iron metals!,

Big red-lettered SYKE,
In the center of SYKE Park on display!,
Placed up on a pedestal,
For "so-called" love's decay,

AND...

(LOOKATCHA' NOW!!!)...(JUST LOOK AT YOURSELF!!!)...

GUILTY of being TOO QUICK,
TO PUT that nigga or bitch,
High up on a shelf!,

PUT that nigga or bitch,
HIGH up on a pedestal,
JUST like the SYKE Park Sculpture,
MADE from the WORST,
OF cast iron metals!,

You THOUGHT you were in love!,
YOU drank the Kool-Aid,
AND believed ALL the HYPE!!,

UNTIL...

(YOU asked that nigga or bitch, if they loved you back?)...

AND...

(THEY LAUGHED RIGHT DEAD IN YOUR FACE!!!)...

And(said)...

"Yeah, I love you,...SYKE!!!"

LOST

THE SON

Those aren't fireflies,
The sun's been raining tears,
The sun's all red from crying,
The sun's been sad for years,

The sun has hung his head,
That's why it sits so low,
The sun has given up,
That's why it sets so slow,

Those aren't fireflies,
The sun's been raining tears,
The sun's all red from crying,
The sun's been depressed for years.

i CAN'T BELIEVE IT'S NOT BUTTER

i met the devil she was packing a pistol,
Skin like glass her name was Crystal,
Shot holes ALL THROUGH my FUCKING NOSE tissue,
My handsome face God DAMN i miss you,

She said I don't care about your looks, I'll still love you so,
Told me she won't care if i go broke, I'll never let me go,
i said BET, i'll FUCK WITH YOU for just a little bit mo',
i think that was six months ago,

We fuck for days with no food, sleep or water,
And i don't speak all i do is mutter,
About how the blood will flow just like hot butter,
When i KILL MY neighbors', mothers, DAUGHTERS and BROTHERS,

She got me SITTIN' in the dark, PEEPING shadows and light,
She got me LISTENING FO' SOUNDS, HOLDING this BIG ASS KNIFE,
She got me down on floor patrol, 'cause her pussy's that tight,
She takes away what haunts me, and has me feeling alright,

i love her JUST LIKE MONEY, i miss her when she's gone,
But when she returns, AIN'T NOTHING is WRONG,
Our love is FUCKED UP, like that WHITE GIRL and KING KONG,
But she's the only girl that loves me, so our love is THAT STRONG,

WHEN i'm WITH HER, the wind don't blow,
The sun don't shine, the moon don't glow,
What day is it? 'CAUSE i DON'T KNOW!,
i'M THE STAR of THIS tragic one-man show.

MY TWO GIRLFRIENDS

I have a girlfriend,
Her name is Crystal,
She burns like a missle,
I have another one,
Her name is Doe,
And when they aren't around,
I miss them so,

I love them when they're here,
And I miss them when they're gone,
The always make me feel good,
And they never do me wrong,

Doe's eyes are green,
Like the color of money,
Crystal can pushback the clouds,
Make a dark day sunny,

No other girl wants me,
So persistantly,
It's just got to be,
Just us three,

So permanently,
My two girlfricnds,
Will be all I need,
Me, meth, and money,
To make all my dark days sunny.

SUCK MY DICK

Have you heard nothing?,
They're trying to help you dude,
MAYBE I don't want to hear,
MAYBE this is WHAT I WANT to do,
Destroy myself before I get sick,
Heart disease can suck my dick,

So I drink,
And drive my motorcycle fast in the rain,
I'm invincible,
I can take your pain,
I'm tough as nails,
I'm tough as shit,
But diabetes can suck my dick,

And before I die,
If I have any hair,
I'll grow dreads down to my underwear,
With Proverbs 15:3 tatted under my eyes,
'Cause it won't matter when I die,
Speaking of death,
Yo cancer check this,
You can come and suck my dick.

I HOPE ALL THIS WEED KILLS ME

Gonna have a heart attack,
Gonna have a heart attack,
Gonna have a heart attack,
Brought on by smoking a pound of weed,
Had to put the Bible down,
'Cause my head is to full to feed,
And I think Jesus turned his back on me,
'Cause I ain't perfect like I'd like to be,

But I tried,
But it wasn't good enough,
So it's take a drink and take a puff,
And take a drink and take a puff,
And take a drink and take a puff,
And I hope all that gives me a stroke,
I want my head to explode,
(That AIN'T NO joke!),

And THIS TIME when I die,
I hope I'm sentenced to death,
Like I committed a crime,
And I hope I can't see,
And I hope I can't think,
And I don't want to see black,
And I don't want to sink,

And unlike last time,
(Being the first time that I died),
I REALLY DO HOPE that THIS TIME,...
It's nothing.
No black.

No light.
No thought.
No sight.

MORNING PISS

Ain't nuthin' LIKE waking up,
On the kitchen floor!,
(Oh, YOU KNOW,
YOU HAVE done THAT before!),

Doing so,
The next day,
Into the bathroom,
He makes his way,

With head back,
And with eyes closed,
And with the odor,
(of and from),
The strain,
(of and from),
The pressure,
(of and from),
The pain,
(of and from),
The pleasing-release,
(of and from),
A strong and long morning piss,
(pissin' out a bottle of that brown liquor!),
(OF AND FROM!),
A HEALTHY-DOSE,
WAFTING-THE-FUCK,
UP HIS NOSE!!,

And(WITH THAT!)...

(It's like gettin' hit with a bat!)...

Like...

Some kind of delayed-reaction,
(of and from),
Gettin' hit in the nuts!,
(of and from),
The pushin',
(and, of),
The straining,
(OF AND FROM!!),
Nutsack-impact-retraction!!,
GOT his head starting to pound!,

And...

IT'S GOT HIM,
WANTING TO bite,
The mutha' fuckin' dog,
THAT bit him!,

And so...

He heads towards the kitchen,
To have a look around!,...

(Oh please believe, THAT he was MOST PLEASED!!!)...

FOR...

A skull-topped bottle of Padre Azul,
Is what he found!,...

"*AHHHH,* the things we do to ourselves!",
(Is what he, says),...

After…

He poured some out for his beloved dead,
'Bout to get bodied,
After he removed the skull from the body,
After getting "bodied",
After taking that skull's forgotten about body,
To the head!

BREAK TIME'S OVER (THE CITY OF CRACKHEADS AND SHATTERED DREAMS - PRELUDE)

The prostitutes getting grinded on by the bitches,
Getting grinded-on by the hookers,
Getting grinded-on by the hoes,
Getting grinded on their backs,
All hustle off the bed,
To get back on their hustle,
And back on their grind.

THE CITY OF CRACKHEADS AND SHATTERED DREAMS

Up on the tenth-floor,
Looking for more,
Down on floor patrol,
She lost her soul,
Down on her hands and knees,
Begging God please,
More scabs than scars,
Crystal blue eyes in the stars,
Shit and blood on the walls,
Face contorted and jawed,
Keep an eye for the law,
And for a bag of that raw,

Smokin', sniffin', drinkin', stinkin',
Ten bucks, five bucks, one buck, Lincoln,
Hookers and drug dealers winkin',
Red and blue cop lights blinkin',
Out in "The Cut" rollin' wit this hooker in tight leather,
Heather's makin' that money in ANY kind of weather!,
If we die tonight - We die together,
HOPE I die tonight - It's whatever,

Homeless, addicts, hookers and nuts,
Pimps, pushers, players and us,
Out in "The Cut" better have NO trust!,
AND stay ready FOR a face to bust!,

Rocks and white lines,
Bumps and light dimes,
30's and Perc 5's,
Vodka and cheap wine,

Chasing death and a good grind,
All in the name of a good time!,
Up at the end of the line,
It's the land of the lost,
Me, D, and Heather,
On our tenth-floor Holocaust.

THE STREETS ARE UNDEFEATED

The streets are undefeated,
So does it make any sense?,
Trying to make a dollar,
Outta fifteen cents?,

Each and every day,
We put our lives on the line,
Trying to make a dollar,
Outta nickle and a dime,

And(FOR WHAT?!?)...

'Cause...

It really doesn't make NO sense!,

'Cause...

NOBODY ever won!,

'CAUSE...

WE ALWAYS stay up under the streets' and the cops' gun!!!,

RATHER...

It's seeking - Yet NOT finding!,
Looking for...THAT silver lining!,

And(Yet!)...

Between the politicians - friends - and policemen,...

(Guess what???)...

EVERYBODY'S LYING!!!,

AND SO...

What WE have ARE homes IN a row!,
Hookers AND hoes!!,
Heroin AND blow!!!,
UT-OH!!!!,...HERE. WE. MUTHA'. FUCKIN'. GO!!!!!,...

Born in the ghetto,
With nowhere to go,
Four-block radius,
The streets ARE chasing us!,

Who was it that said,
The only thing constant,
In this world is change?,
Yet, in the ghetto,...

(Guess what???)...

EVERYTHING REMAINS THE SAME!!!,

AND SO...

WE STAY trying to make a dollar,
Outta fifteen cents!,

But(YET!)...

It's like a penny with a hole in it,...
IT DON'T make no cents!,

And(THAT'S why!)...

Day by day WE fight!,
WE kick, WE scream!!,

But(Yet)...And(BUT STILL!!)...

Day by day there ain't,

No change THROUGHOUT the scene!,

For(YOU SEE!!)...

The streets are undefeated!,
Same old fight,
But just a different round,...

AND...

It's got US feeling like,
There ain't no place to go but down!,

All our dreams, our hopes,
All our wishes for the best,
Enter the doors of institutions,
Jail, or death,

'Cause...

The streets are undefeated,
Yes, I really mean it!,
I said, the streets are undefeated,
The streets are undefeated,

WE never won,
WE'RE always up under the gun,
The "game" AIN'T a game,...

AND...

Ain't NOBODY won!,

SOOOOOO...

Whatchu' doin' on somebody's streets?,
On somebody's stoop?,
On somebody's steps?,

All under the illusion OF inclusion,
That YOU'RE gonna be the one,
Able TO pass the streets' test!,

For(YOU SEE!!)...

The streets are undefeated!,
Ain't nobody got the best of them yet!,
FOOL, DON'T YOU KNOW???,...
There AIN'T no "Old Timers Day",
FOR them "street nigga" vets!!!,

And...

If you REALLY 'bout that "game"?,
YOU in that "game" for life!,

For(YOU SEE!!)...
From the streets there AIN'T NO retirement,
EVEN IF you're living right!,

'Cause...

The streets WILL come for ya'!,
Grip you up in the middle of the night!!,
Blast you in ya' chest!!!,
Sex slave ya' kids and ya' wife!!!,

'CAUSE...

The streets ARE undefeated!,
Yes, I REALLY mean it!!,
I said, the streets ARE undefeated!!!,
THE. STREETS. ARE. UNDEFEATED.

MIRROR, MIRROR

Mirror, mirror,
On the sink,
Who's the dopest boy u think?,

The mirror said, you ask all the time,
Now shut up and do up, these two fat lines,

Mirror, mirror,
On the sink,
Who's the dopest boy u think?,

The mirror said, u is fool,
Now do up these lines, 'cause ur super cool,

Mirror, mirror,
On the sink,
Who's the dopest boy u think?

The mirror said, u is nigga,
U get the banging chicks, with the ghetto figure,

Mirror, mirror,
On the sink,
Who's the dopest boy you think?,

The mirror said, u the dopest one,
Now snort up this, son ma' gun,

Mirror, mirror,
On the sink,
Who's the dopest boy u think?,

The mirror said, who do u think?
U see ur reflection in me, but never blink,

Mirror, mirror,
On the sink,
Who's the dopest boy u think?

The mirror said, u ask all the time,
Now shut up and do up, these two fat lines.

BROKEN SHATTERED MAN

Able to self-diagnose,
The symptom of the growth,
Of his aggravation,
By the formation,
Of tightness at the back of his throat,

He already knows the deal,
With his actions,
Of his thought process surpassing,
He pulls back,
A fistful of glass quills,

As...

The broken shattered self,
Of the broken shattered image,
Of his broken shattered self,
Looks back at his broken shattered self,
Of his broken shattered self,
Looking at his broken shattered image,
Of his broken shattered self,
Looking at his broken shattered self,
Looking at his broken shattered self,
Looking at his broken shattered self,
Looking back at his broken shattered self,
Within the broken shattered image,
Within the broken shattered bathroom mirror,
Looking back at his broken shattered self,
Standing there,

Standing there,

Bobbing and weaving,
Side to side,
To and fro,
Takes more than that to see a change,
The man is broken,

Standing there,
The broken shattered man,
Fully caught up in the whirlwind,
Attempts to gain clarity,
Of his broken shattered self within,
The broken shattered bathroom mirror,
Of his broken shattered image,
Looking back at the broken shattered man,
Standing there,
With blood streaming and dripping,
From the fistful of glass quills,
Embedded in his hand,

Standing transfixed,
In a staring contest,
Of disassociation,
Therein,

He stares back at himself,
Of himself,
Still staring back at him,
Having no idea which one is he in?,

His precognition,
Of his ocular physical disposition,
Is not what he finds,

As...

It occurs to him,
What looks like him,
Stares back at him,
Through broken mirror lines,

Him,
Yet, not himself,
Yet, himself,
Still,

Neither,
Of which,
Are capable to feel,
The pain of a fistful of glass quills,

He lowers his head,
And closes his eyes,
And takes a deep breath,
If he could only exhale it all away,
He tries,

On the sink his hands bear his weight,
Bloodied-quill-drippings run down the drain,
Can't run from himself,
Feeling drained,
His head rises yet once again,

With a vail of tears set in his eyes,
Himself,
Looking back at his blurry self,
Can still see all the pain,
He's been trying to hide,

Both shattered and broken,

The one in the mirror can see within him,
There's still hope and,
It's up to the one standing there,
To recognize that spark to be awoken,

For...

Both of them,
The one within,
And the one,
Standing in front,
One has placed them both in a position,
That neither of them want,

Be it destiny,
Or be it fate,
Both now stand in a mirror,
In which,
Within which,
Seven years of bad luck,
Are about seven years too late!,

Shattered,
Not fragile,
Broken,
Still agile,
No smoke in this mirror,
Authentically magical,
Floating, no feather,
No let up,
Get better,
The broken shattered man inside,
Watches the broken shattered man with pride,

As...

He watches himself,
Piece themselves,
Back together.

PEER PRESSURE

Pulling hard,
On the black twisted wrought iron door handle,
The heavy wooden door creaks open,
For nothing more,
Than to see if he can handle,

The pitch-black room,
Spinning on a downward loop,
Nauseates the legions in the club,
Suffering passed out on the floor,

The hangers-on,
Who thought they could hang,
Hang onto strength of brighter days,
Before the nauseating spinning-darkness,
Welcomes them in,

In the girls,
Lights and drinks,
Above the lost that lost grip,
The indifference,
Of the party that continues,
Is the reality of the hangers-on,
Who couldn't hang,

Stepping over,
The partiers passed out,
Down on the floor,
He steps past the partiers,
Getting down on the floor.

Walking past,

The hangers-on still hanging,
The bartender gives him a drink to be pounded,
As he gives the bartender a pound,

With his eyes,
On the door to exit,
He peers over the peer pressure,
As it appears as though,
The party is over,

Figuring out,
The formula of how,
To handle the labyrinth formed of figures,
He reaches for the handle,
As he reaches the front door,

Pushing,
The door forward,
And stepping outside,

He watches,
As the next wave,
Of hangers-on,
Pushes forward,

Starving,
For heavy servings,
Of discounted beverages,
Made from barley,

Shamelessly eager,
To enter these haunts,
The lost tidal wave surges forward,
As the riptide of spirits,
Thirsts of its dark-spinning loop,

Concurrent,
To the current,
As the riptide pulls the lost under,
To the side he stands aware,
Knowing there ain't nothing,
But peer pressure in there.

THE WELL

Looking on...

In: Silent - I-Know-He's-JUST-Makin'-Up-Shit-
On-The-Fly-With-That-"SALES-PITCH"-
But-I-Know-He's-Right-EVEN-IF-
TO-BE-The-Case-HE-Don't-Know-It-
But-To-Be-The-Case-I-KNOW-It-
And-I-Should-Know-Better-
And-I-Know-I-Know-Better-
And-I-Know-I-Know-I-SHOULD-DO-Better-
BUT-I-WANT-To-Stand-In-Good-Stead-
SO-INSTEAD-I'LL-JUST-Nod-My-Head-
IN: "Silent-Agreement" - type of - Silent Agreement!,

FOR...

The world needs ditch-diggers,
And head-nodders too!,
(Nothin' wrong with being a ditch-digger!)...

For(YOU SEE!!!)...

"CERTAIN PEOPLE" festor 'round AND upon,
Like a bloodlogged leach in a pond,
NEED and require,
The: Silent-Head-Nodding-
In-Agreement-
Silent-Head-Nodders!,

OF...

("Signing-on" AND selling out!!),...

TO...

Feel special!,

AND...

(WITHOUT a doubt!),...

TO...

Feel superior!,

For(You See)...

(Thee: "Attention:Love Ratio" - IS inferior!),...

AND SO...

To: "PUMP the love",
(fuck the heart!),
Into THEIR OWN heads!,

For(YOU SEE!!!)...

(It's the ONLY thing that makes "CERTAIN PEOPLE" NOT TO feel dead!!!)...

So(THAT!)...

They CAN carry-on,
(in, Their: "shallow-bullshit-lives"),
With NO let up OR slack!!,

SO(THAT!!)...

(IN, Their: "shallow-bullshit-lives"),
They CAN feel better 'bout,
What they KNOW they lack!,
SO(THAT!!!)...

They are able, TO: "Justify the Bullshit"!,
(AND this NEXT PART UPON YOU,
SHOULDN'T come UNTO YOU,
As ANY form of amazements!),...
BUT MOST are JUST TO far gone and removed,
FROM, The: "Requirement of The Justifications"!,

'Cause...

("CERTAIN PEOPLE" ARE THAT shallow!!!)...

'Cause...

("CERTAIN PEOPLE'S" hearts ARE THAT hollow!!!)...

'Cause...

(THESE "CERTAIN MUTHAFUCKAS" ARE a trip!!!)...

FOR(YOU SEE!!!)...

They live,
RETURN TO,
Bathe, eat,
AND provide nutrients,
From, THAT: Bottomless -
Three Toad -
Swarmin' Of Green-Backed Flies -
"Well of Bullshit"!!!,

For(You See)...

"CERTAIN PEOPLE" WILL be,
ALL TOO pleased,...
Of saying, WHAT THEY said,
AND OF, HOW it WAS said!,
TO "pullout" FROM YOU,

The MUCH Coveted:
"Silent-In-Agreement-Head-Nodding-Of-The-Head!",

And...

(WHY is that, YOU may ask?)

Well...

(I'LL FUCKING TELL YOU!!!)...

'CAUSE...

As, far as, "CERTAIN PEOPLE" ARE concerned,
IF THEY CAN get just ONE or TWO,
(Though, preferably, EVERYONE in the room!!!),
OF: "Their Bullshit" - TO: "buy into",...

AND(THAT!)...

They MADE YOU "give and provide",
(EVEN IF,...YOU KNOW IT'S a lie!),
That they MADE YOU "OFFER-UP",
The: "Silent-Head-Nod-Of-Agreement - BUTTER-UP"!!!,...

And(FOR This!)...

(OF, The: GETTING people TO buy into "THEIR Bullshit"!!),
"CERTAIN PEOPLE" WILL believe,
(scratch that!)...("CERTAIN PEOPLE" DON'T think!!!),...

FOR...

"CERTAIN PEOPLE" KNOW!,
"CERTAIN PEOPLE" KNOW HOW!!,...
TO: KNOW THAT THEY ARE,...
ON TOP of "THEIR GAME" RIGHT now!!!,

And(FOR That!)...

"CERTAIN PEOPLE" can do NO wrong!,
Yanking YOUR chain WITH THEIR "SALES-PITCH"!!,
IN the form, OF: A dance. And a song.

And(FOR THAT!!!)...

WHAT "CERTAIN PEOPLE" COVET,
THE MOST - ALL THE TIME,
IS THEIR NEED TO BE,
FULLY IN LOVE WITH,
THEIR: "FAST - ROCKETSHIP -
POWERFUL - I - THINK-I'M-WONDERFUL -
(((FUCK-YOUR-FEELINGS!!!))) -
NEXT-HUSTLE/NEW-HUSTLE - MIND"!!!,

For(You See)...

Be it out in the streets,
Or perched-up high upon a throne,
(Of tufted leather upholstered!),
There's JUST NO END TO "CERTAIN PEOPLE'S bullshit"!!!,
AND "THEIR BULLSHIT" upon YOU,
THEY are ALWAYS READY AND WILLING to unholster!,

For(YOU SEE)...

TO "CERTAIN PEOPLE",
Be it out on the corner,
YOUR FEELINGS are a goner!,
OR perched-up high upon a throne,
YOUR feelings ARE YOUR OWN!!,

FOR(YOU SEE!!!)...

"CERTAIN PEOPLE" will lose NO sleep,
From NOT knowing IF upon YOU,
THEY WENT to "The Well" TOO deep!,

And...

(WHAT-ON-EARTH "Well" IS THAT, YOU may ask??)

Well...

(Hang on tight!)

AS...

(I perform THIS "Public Service" task!),...

THAT stinkin', Well.
That bottomless, unrelenting,
uncaring and endless, Well.
That swarmin' of green-backed flies, Well.
That parasitic, Well.
That maggots-and-brain-eatin'-amoebas -
molds - and three toads, Well.
(Swimmin', livin', down deep,
down in the mystery-waters of THAT bullshit, Well),
THAT WELL!!!
(YOU KNOW THAT WELL!!!),...
(DON'T ACT LIKE YOU DON'T!!!),...

THAT WELL!!!!!!

THAT Well,...

Packed with nothin' but LIES and BULLSHIT, WELL!!!!!!

(THAT'S THE MOTHERFUCKIN' WELL,
MOTHERFUCKERS!!!!!!)

That Well,
The shiesty, "out-for-me-and-fuck-you's",
(of the world),
Use and use you,
To build their homes,
Clothe their children and,
Feed their fuckin' kids from, Well.
The Well, their kids (essentially) feed directly out of, Well.
The Well, they feed their kids directly out of, Well.
(Yes,...THAT Well!!!!!!).

And(WITH That!)...

"CERTAIN PEOPLE" WITH bated breath will wait,...
TO SEE IF YOU took the bait!,
That being: A 30 gallon steel drum,
Attatched to a great rusty chain,
That burn barrel is hung,...

AND...

Inside of it,
Is the "SALES-PITCH",
Being hoisted-up from the depths in which,
Comes deep down from within,
THAT "Well Of Bullshit"!,

And...

ALONG WITH that 30 gallon steel drum,
They wait with bated breath to see,
IF YOU ARE BEING HOISTED-UP!!!,

For(You See!)...

"CERTAIN PEOPLE" NEED to know,
IF they are ON TOP of "Their Game",
AS on THAT big rusty chain they give a big yank,
(AS WITH the subsequent "yanking of YOUR chain"!),
From the depths of "THAT WELL",
That burn barrel does so rise,...

FOR(YOU SEE!!)...

OF WHICH - IN WHICH,
CONTAINING CONTENTS -
OF: GREEN-BACKED FLIES -
AND - ENDLESS BULLSHIT!!!,
OF WHICH - IN WITH -
THE BRAIN-EATING-WORMS -
THERE'S NOTHING "CERTAIN PEOPLE" WOULD,
LOVE MORE - FROM YOU - THAN TO LEARN -
OF YOU - FROM YOU - TO CONFIRM -
OF YOU - FROM YOU - IF YOU - WOULD BE SO INCLINDED -

FOR(YOU SEE!!!)...

("CERTAIN PEOPLE" NEED TO KNOW)...

If...

YOU ARE INSIDE!!!

AAAAAAND...

(HOW-ON-EARTH WOULD "CERTAIN PEOPLE" KNOW THAT???)...

(YOU may ask;)

Well...

(I'LL FUCKING TELL YOU!!!)...

BY...

"Offering-up",
The: MOST COVETED -
Silent-In-Agreement-Head-Nodding-Of-The-Head -
THAT YOU provide!

(AND FUCK YOUR FEELINGS MOTHERFUCKERS!!!)...(DON'T BE, A: Silent-In-Agreement-Head-Nodder-Of-The-Head!).

GREEN 'ROUND THE GILLS

Narcissistic delusional diluted,
THIS fool's brain was SO polluted,
Green gills filtered bong waters filled,
With mustard green hash, narcotics,
And cough syrup flavored-vermouth,

The professional bridge burner,
The steadily clout-chasin'-claimin'-never-earner,
Was NEVER gonna follow thru,
His NEXT "boo-hoo" IS HIS excuse,

Couldn't hold down a job,
Couldn't hold it together,
Couldn't care less about his kids,
Couldn't care less to uphold the word of truth.

IT'S ALWAYS RUNNY IN PHILADELPHIA

This one right-here,
Doesn't curse or fib,
He don't even talkback to his parents,
Or give them any lip,...

Let's shoot him dead!

This one right-here,
Goes to school everyday,
And doesn't skip,
This girl right-here,
Is a good kid,...

Let's shoot her dead!

This one right-here,
Stayed on track,
And didn't slip,
NOW he's got,
A full-ride football scholarship,...

Let's shoot him dead!

This one right-here,
Works two jobs,
To feed her kids,
Six bus transfer workday trip,...

Let's shoot her dead!

This one right-here,
Perservered,
The nerve of him,

He started his own biz,
After serving a 10-year bid,...

Let's shoot him dead!

You WON'T believe,
What this one right-here,
Is trying to achieve,...

He's PROUD of his hood!,
(Did I fail to mention?),
THIS FOOL right-here,
WANTS TO make a difference!,...

Let's shoot him dead!

This one right-here,
Isn't about sillyness,
PLUS she claims to be,
Allergic to ignorance!,...

Let's shoot him dead!

This one right-here,
Dresses different,
This one right-here,
MUST THINK he's different!,

Let's shoot him dead!

This one right-here,
Reads books and she has,
Constructive hobbies,
This one wants to be somebody,...

Let's shoot her dead!

She's at a high school football game,

This one right-here's not bothering nobody,
Be a shame if during the game,
She became a dead body,...

Let's shoot her dead!

His mommy got shot,
Now he's the mommy,
If not, his sisters would be orphans,
Probably,...

Let's shoot him dead!

For(You See)...

The ones through life that tread,
WITH one MUST strive IN life IN their head,
Knows WHAT it takes,
TO get ahead!,

And...

The ones that tread with HATE,
Knows what IT takes,
And THAT'S a weak head,
TO SHOOT 'EM DEAD!!!

IT ABSORBS

And so...

His thoughts,
And actions,
HAVE BEEN sloooooowed down!,

As(with)...

(The sounds - Within - The scene - Within - YOUR TUMBLIN' car!),...

IN WHICH...

(Therein - THERE'S PLENTY of YOUR car's contents - FLOATIN' 'round!!),...

AS(WITH)...

(Within - The Room - HE'S - Within!),...

AS...

(YOU REMAIN hog-tied and HELPLESS - RUMBLIN' TOWARDS YOUR DOOM!!!),...

In any rate...

(MAKE NO MISTAKE - THIS PLACE is fuckin' weird!),...

FOR(YOU SEE!!!)...

HIS shadow moves,
IN slooooow-motion time!,

FOR...

HIS sight and sounds,

HAVE BEEN slooooowed down!!,...

AS(WITH)...

(YOUR screechin' tires - ENROUTE TO A DEER!!!!),...

In any rate...

(MAKE NO MISTAKE - It's his shadow that AIN'T),...

GOT NOTHIN' to do wit his mind,
TELLIN' his vision THAT EVERYTHIN',
IS movin' IN slooooow-motion time!!,

AS(WITH)...

(THAT impending bridge abutment IMPACT - TUMBLIN' in a car - YOU CAN NOT STEER!!!!),...

For(You See)...

HIS OWN weird-shadow casts,
UPON the white wall he faces,...

AND...

(MAKE NO MISTAKE - It's HIS shadow that AIN'T),...

Got NOTHIN' to do wit the flicker,
Of a candle's flame!,

AND...

(MAKE NO MISTAKE - It's HIS shadow that AIN'T),...

Got NOTHIN' to do wit what his,
Eyeballs ARE seeing from his brain!!,

For(You SEE)...

HE SEES his shadow from cross the room,
With his right hand,
Of it,
He traces,...

And...

IT IS WHAT HE SEES,
His heart,
Of it,
Right hand he places!,

FOR(YOU SEE)...

HIS SHADOW,
IN REAL-TIME,
IT REFUSES TO MOVE!,
OUTTA' SHEAR AND BLATANT-DEFIANCE!!!,

RATHER...

IN sloooooow-motion-moves,...(((IT MORPHS!!!))),
HIS SHADOW,...IS DELAYED!!!,
OUTTA' SHEAR - AND - IN PURE -
HUMANLY-NONCOMPLIANCE!!!!!!,

For(YOU SEE!!)...

UPON the wall he faces,
(to be sure!),
HIS shadow,
IT laps LIKE the ocean,...
UPON the sands of the shore!,

AS...

He watches,...

On the wall,...
The shadow,...
Of his arm,...
REFUSING TO FUSE,...
In, and of,
The body-shadow,
IN real-time,
His shadow-arm,
IS STILL NOT...APART!!!,

OF WHICH...

(OF COURSE - WOULD BE - OF THE NATURAL TREND!!!)

RATHER...

(ON IT'S OWN TIME!!!)...

The shadow,...
On the wall,...
OF HIS OWN ARM,...
Does so,...
AS IT DOES SO,...
Moving towards,...
In, and of,
The body-shadow,...
IT slooooowly bends!!!,

And...

UPON the wall he faces,
(TO BE SURE!),
His shadow,...
IT laps LIKE the ocean,...
UPON the sands of the shore!,

FOR...

(JUST LIKE WITH!)...
An ocean's breakers' remnants,...
            His shadow,...
                Slooooowly filters down,...
                    As IT absorbs!,...

In any rate...

(MAKE NO MISTAKE - THIS PLACE is fuckin' weird!),...

FOR(YOU SEE!!!)...

HIS shadow moves,...
IN slooooow-motion time!,...

FOR...

HIS sight and sounds,...
HAVE BEEN slooooowed down!!,...

AS(WITH)...

(YOUR screechin' tires - ENROUTE TO A DEER!!!!).

WE IS WHERE WE AT

We is where we at,
As a matter of fact,
I ran over the Cuckoo's Nest,
You got that Jack?,

In league with the Cat In The Hat,
Madder than The Hatter,
I've been through Hell,
And now I'm back!,

We're all addicts and drunks,
In our own ways,
And we all fall down,
On different days,

We weren't put on this earth to judge,
So don't do that,
And I thank God,
We is where we at!,

This one gives no resistance,
And this one doesn't listen,
And this one left rehab,
'Cause the drugs she was missing,

This one is real,
And this one is whack,
One can't read,
And this one is black,

This one can spit,
And this one can rap,
This one is nuts,

And this one smokes crack,

This one tells jokes,
And this one drinks Jack,
This one plays cards,
And this one bangs smack,

This one can't write,
And this one talks back,
This one is white,
And this one lives in a shack,

This one sniffs powder,
This one knows facts,
This one totted a burner,
He made it click-clack,

And this one lives in his van,
He's just here for the snacks,
He's just runnin' a scam,
Faked another O.D. so that he could come back,

We is where we at,
As a matter of fact,
And I RAN over the Cuckoo's Nest,
You got that Jack?,

And I'm in league with The Cat In The Hat,
And I'm Madder THAN The Hatter,
Please believe I've been through HELL,
NOW it feels LIKE I'm back!,

And we IS where WE at,
AS a matter of fact!,
AND I thank God every day,
We is WHERE we at!

CAUGHT *FEELINGS?*

(Psst!)...(Hey reader!)...

Have YOU ever had that *FEELING,*
Of not quite being scared?,
That *FEELING* of waking up,
Where upon you A DEEP sleep crept,...
Where subsequently YOU so slept,...
WHERE YOU SLEPT,...
FOR...the... *VERY...FIRST...TIME!!!,*
THAT *FEELING* of, "Ok,...I think,...
I'm in a safe place.",...
But,...WHERE the fuck am I???",...

And...(With THAT *FEELING!),...*

THAT - crashed-in-someone's-back-guest-room-
after-a-night-of-heavy-drinking - *FEELING,*
THAT - just-opening-your-eyes-
and-not-seeing-anything-that-
looks-like-your-own - *FEELING!,*
THAT - waking-up-and-not-seeing-
anything-that-looks-familiar - *FEELING,*

(((THAT - EXTRA-tired - *FEELING!!!)))*

THAT - *FEELING* YOU GET,
When you first wake up,
And you're SO DAMN TIRED,
(YET slept so sound!),
That UPON opening your eyes,
FOR the very first time,

(SINCE YOU laid-it-on down!),
THAT YOU involuntarily start blinking,
(AND in doing so!),...
YOU CAN *FEEL* YOUR EYES STINGING!!,

Yeah...(((THAT *FEELING!!!)))*

And...(((WITH that *FEELING!!!)))...*

THAT - *FEELING* of IF in fact,
IF by blinking you're not sure,
IF you're actually causing your,
Eyelids to start stinging,
By together bringing,
When you're blinking??,
Or IF it's actually your eyeballs??,
IF THAT'S actually what's stinging??,

'Cause...(((THAT *FEELING* got you unsure!!!)))

AND...(((WITH THAT *FEELING!!!)))...*

BY blinking all that you're REALLY doing,...
Is cause for thee ensuing,
Stinging of the eyeballs,...
TO sting EVEN more!!,

(Damned if you DO!)...and...(Damned if you DON'T - type-shit!!)...

For(You See)...

Upon awakening this way you may find,
You beez in a true no-win situation!,

For...

It beez that way sometimes,
And sometimes it beez that way!,

For...

Upon awakening this way you may find,
You beez in a state of contemplation!!,

So...

(Fuck it!)...

SOMETIMES it goes that way,
AND sometimes THAT'S JUST the way it goes!,

For(YOU See!)...

YOU might as well stay the fuck in THAT bed,
WITH your motherfuckin' eyes closed!!,

Yeah...(((THAT *FEELING!!!)))...*

And...(((WITH THAT *FEELING!!!)))...*

One can't shake THAT *FEELING* so easy!,
THAT - *FEELING* of, "I could sleep another 5-6 hours easy!",

'Cause...(HEY!)...

WITH your eyes closed at the VERY least,
The stinging of your eyes OR your lids,
(AS the case MAY BE!!)...WILL cease!!,

REGARDLESS...

(Of WHY they're stinging!!)

REGARDLESS...

(Of WHICH ONES are actually DOING the stinging!!)

IRREGARDLESS...

(((THAT *FEELING* - IS SNEAKY!!!)))

'CAUSE...(Guess what?)...

"FUCK!!!",
Sneaking in,...in time,...

It's NOW you realize,
THAT *FEELING* has - "snuck-it" - INTO your head!!!,
THAT, "Oh shit! THIS ain't MY bed!!!,...
And...WHERE the fuck AM I again???",...

Yeah...(((THAT fucked-up *FEELING!!!)))...*

THAT *FEELING* of, "Damn! I must'uv REALLY been OUT!!!",...

'Cause...

"MY EYES HAVEN'T STUNG LIKE THIS",...

SINCE...

"The LAST TIME I woke up SO tired LIKE THIS!!",...

YET...

"Slept SO sound!!!",...

THAT - waking-up-your-freshmen-year-of-college-
for-the-first-time-in-your-dorm-room-BEFORE-you-
can "fig'a-it-all-out" - *FEELING!!!,*

THAT *FEELING* of emotion,
Of THAT moment,

YOU just woke up,
And TO get it ALL-worked-out in YOUR mind,...
IT TAKES YOU a few-sleepy-moments!,

Yeah...(((THAT *FEELING!!!)))*

(Psst!)...(Hey reader!)...

HAVE YOU ever CAUGHT *FEELINGS???*

FOUND

SANCTATURIUM

Downstairs, all alone,
I'm renting this house, so it ain't no home,
But downstairs, by myself,
I have a room, all to myself,

On the walls, photos of family and friends,
Everywhere you look, Silver and Black again,
Down here to find peace, my escape,
I like being alone, my little place,

Sanctuary, a place to get well,
Sanaturium, a place of living hell,
This is my Sanctaturium, a combination of both,
Friends please come in, others I'll choke,

I always wanted, a Raider Room,
Finally got it, my Legion of Doom,
Not a good day, not a good night,
I hate this time of year, feeling not right,

Oct. 20, the date of my Dad's birth,
Nov. 26, when he left this earth,
Nov. 30, when he was buried,
And Christmas is coming, should I be merry?,

Fuck Thanksgiving, it's not the same,
I miss my Dad, can I be blamed?,
So for little girl, I'll hang up some lights,
Put up a tree, and fake being alright,

No Thanksgiving, at my brother's,
No Christmas dinner, at my Mother's,
Little girl can go, I hope she has fun,
This year I'm staying home, with this bottle of rum,

I'll be downstairs, all alone,
I'll be downstairs, in my headphones,
I'll be downstairs, with no phone,
I'll be downstairs, in my Sanctaturium.

LONE WOLF LIFE

FUCK IT...

I'll be a LONE WOLF for LIFE...

Got no wife,
'Cause I'm TOO damn TRIFE!!,
A loving touch or two,
Would make EVERYTHING alright,
But I'M GOOD right here,
With these PILLS AND THIS KNIFE!!,

It's a HELL of a life...

Self-recluse JUST out of spite!,
Curtains are drawn,
AIN'T NEVER NO light,
You NEVER hear me walk,
WHEN I come out at night,
Shoulda stayed home,
PROBABLY get in a fight!,

FUCK IT...

I'M LIVIN' THE LONE WOLF LIFE!!!

Got "LONE WOLF" carved across my knuckles,
DID IT with a SOUP CAN LID just for chuckles,
GOT BLOOD ALL OVER my ol' belt buckle,
You FUCKIN' with a Lone Wolf?,
You fuckin' WITH trouble!,

(WHAT'S the "Lone Wolf Life"???)...

(ARE YOU READY for THIS??)...

DEPRIVED of love AND a soft kiss!!

BUT...

Watches for snakes and DOESN'T take shit!,
Stays sharp LIKE a slit wrist,
NEVER HAPPY, ALWAYS PISSED,

AND...

A Lone Wolf DON'T ASK FOR SHIT!!!

Long boring days,
Thinking too much,
Keeps pushing hard,
But not in a rush,
Stays downwind,
And paranoid of TRUST,
And CRAVES BLOOD and female lust!,

A Lone Wolf gets FUCKED UP to PASS THE TIME,
A Lone Wolf AIN'T SCARED of the BOX OF PINE,
A Lone Wolf TAKES CARE OF WHAT'S MINE,
A Lone Wolf STAYS READY to fight or grind,

A Lone Wolf gets fucked up in the afternoon,
Death for a Lone Wolf is NEVER too soon,
A Lone Wolf gets lost in his tunes,
And you DAMN RIGHT a Lone Wolf HOWLS at the moon!,

A Lone Wolf AIN'T WORRYING ABOUT being proper,
WANTED BY THE LAW AND MEDICINE DOCTORS,
KEEPS AN EYE OUT for HELICOPTERS,
PROBABLY SEE ME ON THE NEWS for BEATING UP the coppers,

A Lone Wolf is SEPARATED FROM HIS PACK,
SO LIVE EVERY DAY LIKE YOU AIN'T COMING BACK!!!,
EXPECT NONE, and give NO SLACK,
And STAY ready for a FACE to crack!,

A Lone Wolf is hurtin', AND THE WORLD knows,
He TRIES to HIDE IT, BUT it still shows,
And WITH EVERY DAY, HIS pain grows,
LONE WOLF LIFE,...is full of sorrows and woes,

LONE WOLF LIFE is self-preservation,
A LONE WOLF LIVES off the reservation,
A LONE WOLF will TAKE YOUR LIFE with NO HESITATION,
And LIVES the Book of Revelation.

HALLWAY HANNAH

And so...

Once up on his apartment's third-floor,
He found himself,
Kept-on finding himself,
Keeping-on finding,...something more!,

As...

He's finding,...
        IT'S dark and lonely at the top!,
            (IN the darkness of the top floor!),...

UNTIL...

He FINDS,
Once he has finally taken the steps,
And has FINALLY made it to the top,
That he would be confronted,
AND it would be confrontation,
THAT HE is confronted BY!!,

As...

He finds himself,
Finding himself,
Being confronted by,
The self-proclaimed: "Hallway Hannah"!,
(The Apartments' version, of: "profiling-paradigmatics"!),

As...

Hallway Hannah HAS FOUND,
HER SOLE-SELF-RIGHTOUS PURPOSE IN LIFE!,

AND HAS TAKEN IT UPON HERSELF,
To encounter AND enforce the cards SHE'S delt,
OF who's IN THE wrong and WHAT'S RIGHT!,
For(YOU SEE!)...

Hallway Hannah,
NEEDS this confrontation IN her life!,
So THAT she CAN feel IMPORTANT!,
And OF her WILL - OF her confrontations,
Hallway Hannah EXPECTS THE CONFRONTED,...
JUST TO ABSORB IT!,

FOR(YOU SEE!!!)...

HER ENTITLED-ASS,
Feels AS though AND expects,
ANYONE that SHE encounters,...
Just to OBEY!!!,...

As...

Hallway Hannah JUST EXPECTS,
The confronted JUST TO ROLLOVER,
CONFORM TO AND OBLIGE - AS THEY ABIDE,
TO ANY-DAMN-THING SHE SAY!!!,

AND SO...

Hallway Hannah ATTEMPTS to BULLY,
And IMPOSE HER WILL,
Upon ANYONE she feels!,

As...

She feels as though,
ANY ONE of HER "SINGLED-OUT-SCHMOES",
OF their OWN rights - WON'T and DON'T know!!,

And...

(IF ANYONE "happens" to KNOW their rights?)...

Well...

Hallway Hannah FEELS that IT'S HER right,
(OF ANYONE'S RIGHTS) - (of which!),
SHE HAS the right TO REPEAL!!!,

(Psst!)...(Hey, reader!)...

(JUST to make sure WE'RE on the SAME page!!)...

Hallway Hannah's "definition" of: "ANYONE",
Is as follows,...

(Surely she LEARNED from "SOMEONE" thru the ages!),...

ANYONE: That DOESN'T LOOK like her!,
ANYONE: That will MAKE herself FEEL A LOT more superior!,
ANYONE: That DOESN'T LOOK like they BELONG!,
ANYONE: That she SINGLE'S OUT MADE TO FEEL A LOT more inferior!,

(Got it?)...(Good)...(Hang on tight!)...(Psst!)...(Hey, reader)...(LET'S GO!!)...

AND SO...

(As I stated befo')...

Of the third-floor,
Of HIS Apartments,
Tha' brotha made it up to the third-flo',

And...

(Hallway Hannah gets to doing WHAT she do!)...

AS...

Hallway Hannah serves-up,
HER self-serving-bullshit-of-"expertise"!,
"YOU DON'T live here! LET ME see YOUR I.D.!!",

And...

(Hallway Hannah EVEN TOLD the brotha!)...

With her arms spreadout, "I'M CALLING the COPS!!!",
Hallway Hannah demands and commands and,...
Of the brotha's rightful-passage SHE blocks!!!,

Welp...

Hallway Hannah got her nutty-ass mushed in the face!,
Straight-up got mushed straight-down to the floor!,
Straight-up got her nutty-ass stepped-over on his way to HIS door!,...

"YA' FUCKIN' NUT!!!", the brotha yells!,
"I'LL BE IN 'PARTMENT 12!!!!,
CALL THA' FUCKIN' COPS!!!,
AND YOU TELL 'EM FROM ME,
I'LL KEEP THA' DOOR UNLOCKED!!!"

THREE OR MORE

And so...

He sits down on the floor,
(Lotus style),
In and of himself,
To take a look inside,
To gain some clarity,
(As to why?),
He keeps on getting hit with tiny stones,...
Fallen from the sky!,

AND SO...

Of and within,
Of what it is he finds,
Of what it is - it says to him,
That if stones,
Three or more,
Hit you that fell from the sky,

That...

IT'S A CALLING,
(TO BE SURE!!!),
THE PATH is THE ONE of a Shaman,

And...

THAT PATH IS YOURS!!!,

And...

YOU ARE to learn "the ways" to travel,
Between the doors,
TO find the cures!!!

PISS CIRCLE

Lowering his head in revelation,
That his own wit,
Places him in this time-wasting position,
The circulation,
Of frustration,
To infuriation,
By his placement,
Revelation of time,
Unwittingly positioned,
In a circle of waste,
Upon discovery of,
Having been standing atop of blood,
Bull's Eyed in the center circle of,
A liquor-logged urine stain.

LOVE

YOU'RE NOT THE MAN I MET

It's not supposed to be like this,
You're supposed to treat me like your Princess,
You're supposed to take care of me,
You're supposed to marry me,
You're not doing your part,
If I knew you were like this?,
I would not have given you my heart,
And then she told me something I'll never forget,...
"You're not the man I met.",
You're never going to take care of me,
And I know you're never going to marry me,
I group you in with all the rest,
You're supposed to be giving me your best,
Is this why your two wives left you?,
From the same stupid-ass-shit,
You're putting me through?,
And then she told me something I'll never forget,...
"You're not the man I met.",

You're supposed to still take care of me,
You're supposed to still cherish me,
You're supposed to still help me out the shower,
You're supposed to still want to spend with me ever hour,
You used to hold me and say, "Oh you feel so good.",
I shouldn't have to tell you, YOU JUST SHOULD!,
And then she told me something I'll never forget,...
"You're not the man I met.",

The only people that love me, is me and God,
You can never love me, if you don't have LOVE WITHIN, 'Rod',
I'm always alone and we don't go anywhere,
You're supposed to still show me that you care,
You don't do the things you used to do no more,
The summer's almost over,...
AND YOU didn't take me to the shore!,
And then she told me something I'll never forget,...
"You're not the man I met.",

"You're supposed to be my best friend,
The things you used to do,
You're supposed to do them again,
That Boss man I met,
That's who you're still supposed to be,
Maybe I should drive you back to rehab,
I'M taking you back to 'The Roxbury'!,
And then she told me something I'll never forget,...
"You're not the man I met."

THE CHOICE IS SIMPLE

Why hurt the one,
That loves you the most?,
She loves you man!,
SHE'S the one you wanted,
Over two years ago!!,

Treat her right!,
Treat her WITH respect!,
Treat her WITH love!,

Keep everything at an arms distance,
Keep everything out of your aura,
That's irrelivant and negative,

It's the ONLY way!,
It's up to you TO BE happy!,
It's up to you to love yourself again!,

Today's a good day to start,
DON'T destroy the love she has for you!,
DON'T destroy her good heart!,

Be good to her,
Or let her go,
I will be good to you.

TRUTH

You've seen the worst of me,
Now to give you my best,
I've put you through enough,
I must profess,
You've seen the worst of me,
Time to give you my best.

FOREVER HOME

I haven't been a good boyfriend,
Hell, I HAVEN'T been a good friend!,
One bad decision after another,
Would love to start US over again!!,

Gave you EVERY reason to leave me,
Though I never cheated on you,
I gave you every reason TO believe me,
Because my words ARE true!,

You haven't given up on me,
Once in a lifetime soulmates are hard to find,
I don't do all those loving things no more,
Trapped in my head is wasting time,

I do know that you love me,
Maybe you just don't want to be alone,
Just know that your love will always be in my heart,
Your love will always have a home,

Your sweet voice makes me cry,
Your stance and faith on face,
And I always make you cry,
Yet you sooth me with your warm embrace,

How did I get so lucky,
To have you love me as you do?,
Once in a lifetime soulmates are a rare find,
And this I know is true,

The way you sing to me,
Makes us both cry EVERY time!,

Because each time that you sing,
I know YOUR heart is mine!,

And my love for you will ALWAYS be,
My love for you will NEVER roam,
And we'll always live together,
Because my heart is now your home.

THESE ARE MY VOWS TO YOU

To be shown and not told,
To be kind and to hold,
To be adored and not scold,
To love you ‘til I grow old.

FACE-TO-FACE

And so...

(In the living room)...(music cranked hard!)...

She's getting her workout in,
TWERKIN' IT hard!,
THERE'S A knock on the door!,
(She can't hear AND AIN'T trying!),
Her dude calls out, "Babe, GO GET the door!",
(Staying stretched out on the sofa lazily-lying!),

(Hot n' bothered!)...(for him she has a few words!!)...

"Don't SOME PEOPLE have the nerve!,
Tellin' me GO GET the door??,
WHEN YOU'RE the one THAT heard!!",

(Leaving the music blastin'!)...(Trust me holmes - tongues would be waggin'!)...

WITH a walk worthy of braggin'! -
She's JUST-A-THROWIN' THAT wagon! -
Cross the red shag carpet -
She takes her sexy walk cross -
Tight camo leggings WHICH accentuates,
ALL HER STUFF that's bangin'!,

(Made her tour cross the floor)...(she opens the door)...

The sweat on her neck,
And collarbones match,
The dampness on her white tank top,
Just below her boobs,

Is where that shitz cut off!!,
AND ENOUGH to give YOU fits,
Is dampness of her tone midriff!,
DAMMIT! NOW SHE'S JUST PLAIN SHOWING OFF!!!,

(In case you were wondering)...(no bra on:)

Standing there breathing heavily,
Volume still cranked up on her song!,
As she catches her breath,...
She stands there LIKE that,...
AS HE STANDS THERE face-to-face,
LOOKING BACK at her LIKE that!!,

(In the dimness of the hallway)...(at the top of a long set of wooden steps)...

The smell of the building's age in his nose,
And she has a look in her eyes,
"Love me, love me not, Love me, like a rose.",...

(And before him in the doorway)...(WHAT a beautiful sight!)...

He stands there staring into her eyes,
With the ALL-RED-EVERYTHANG lit up behind her,
By bright ambient light!,

(Not seen from his viewpoint)...(lying on the sofa is HER dude!)...

AND OUTTA' THE WAY,
ARE BOTH of their viewpoints!!,

(Both still not saying a single word)...(but as far as they're both concerned)...

Their eyes know what to say,
"We'll both just steal away,

the most of what we know it to be,
A: TORTUROUSLY-BRIEF -
I'm-Going-To-Remember-This-Moment-
For-The-Rest-Of-My-Life -
Moment-In-Time.",

(As they allow)...(the other one)...

To share and be shared,
And to be in that moment with the other.

(As they share that moment)...(together)...

AS SHE,

And so...

All dainty and shit,
Like the strings on her thong,
Two cigars she made love to,
Unlit for too long,
Bedded down in a red marble ashtray,
As she, blew him away,

As she, one at a time,
As she, took her time,
As she, took the liberties,
Of the lighting of both of these,

Tips dipped in sin,
The flame she drew in,
As she, nears masterbation,
As she, reacts to the sweet n' spicy sensation,

Upon her lips,
Next night it won't be him,
Upon a plush red leather love seat,
Her's, not his,
Though, deep seated next to her tonight,
It's his turn to sit,

As she, turns him on,
As she, turns to him,
As she, gives him fits,
As she, begins to wince,

As he, watches her do it,

As she, continues to go through it,
As she, continues to writhe,
Off the sweet n' the spice,

As he's, transfixed by,
The sexy sight,
Of a sexy woman,
With a lit cigar in her hand,
Got him thanking God he's a man,

Busted nuts, busted fathoms,
Rational busted down into irrations,
Regions busting into spasms,
Busted rations of orgasims,
As she, continues her reactions,

As she, leans towards him,
As she, hands him his own sin,
As he, by his,
By from whence of her lips,
Were prior to being placed up to his,

He now knows that sensation,
Though, he does not react,
Nor, act upon,
Wanting to know,...
What her sensation tastes like.

DO YOU WANNA BE MY FUCK UP?

(Do you wanna be my fuck up?)...

And NO I don't think I'm pushin' my luck up!,
'CAUSE with *THAT look* in your eye,
And *THE WAY* you got your bottom lip,
IN your teeth clinched tight!,
I DON'T THINK YOU'RE gonna tell me,
TO shut the fuck up!,

(So?)...(Do you wanna be my fuck up??)...

Yeah, I KNOW you gotta man,
BUT I GOT OTHER PLANS!!!,
Put YOUR hand inside MY hand,
WE both GON' BE FUCKING UP TONIGHT!!!,
YOU understand???,

(So?)...(Tell me)...(Do you wanna be MY fuck up???)...

DEAD LOOKING WOMAN IN HIS ARMS

And...

With car door slammed,
And with him gettin' on his ol' stroll,
(It's FUCK ALL Y'ALL!),
(HE SEES WHAT HE WANTS!!),
HE DON'T GIVE A FUCK 'BOUT TRAFFIC!!!,
Cars nose-divin' - (((*PROCEEDING screeching-tires halts!*))),

As...

(He keeps it pushin' cross the street)...(reaching the sidewalk!)...

FOR...

(He sees her!)...

AND...

(She's oblivious to the sounds!)...

As...

(She stands before and looking up)...

As...

(The Lord's statue at her is looking down!)...

As...

Every day. At this time.
AT High Noon. Rain OR shine.
To the Lord's statue she talks!,

And...

(He's mismerized BY her!)...

AS...

(He takes in her curves!!)...
As...

(He stands there on the sidewalk)...(DIRECTLY BEHIND HER!!!)...

AS...

He CAN'T do ANYTHING but watch!

As...

(Church bells in the distance toll)...(THAT it's High Noon on the clock!!)...

As...

She's well up in the park,...

As...

(She stands upon the gravel and of the stones)...(*Of a former city park bulldozed!)...*

As...

HER beauty, in and of, the rubble,
CREATED AND CREATES a contrast that's stark!,

As...

From him, of her, she's still a good distance,

As...

(FOR him, OF her, he's GOT TO figure out something to say!)...

For...

Upon the sidewalk, he remains frozen.

For...

As a statue, he remains as motionless.

As...

(FOR HIM, he THINKS he knows her)...(BUT he's GOT TO know who!)...

As...

For her, beneath her,
The rocks and rubble, provides her,
With the sweet-discomfort,...of a church pew.

And...

As he approaches, neither one, hear ANY sounds!,
The irate motorists, of the traffic jam he created,
Yields to his heart that pounds!,

As...

His approach to her, draws near.

And...

Of that gravel...

And...

Of those stones...

And...

Of that, of his approach, he hears no tones.

FOR...

As he walks...

(There might as well not even be)...(a surface beneath his feet)...

FOR...

ALL that he CAN hear,...*IS the POUND of HIS heartbeat!*

And...

(That's ALL, that HE, CAN hear!)...

And...

(((DAAAAAAYUM!!!)))...(THERE she is!)...

And so...(HE says to himself)...

"If I'M a gamblin' man?,
I'D BET WE WOULD HAVE,...
Some BEAUTIFUL kids!!",...

AND SO...

From under church bells,
From under sacrilege,
(*From his imaginings!!*),
From his fixed-on-her eyes,
From undressin',
From straight staring her down,
(((Down to HER essence!!!))),
From her soft exposed ankles on up,
From up under that Stetson hat,
He, did so,
As, he persisted,
As such,
From behind sun-blazoned-eyes,

From concluding,...
From being mesmerized!,
OF: HOW. DAAAAAAAYUM!!! TONE.
MUST. BE. HER. THIGHS!! ((OY VEY!!)).

And...

Of her,
SHE TOO,
Persisted!!,
(In, of, and from)...(HER deaf-tunnel-vision-view),...
(Of which)...(At which),...
TO look up,
SHE continued,...

(To all)...

Deaf. Blind. And Mute.

(To all)...(BUT)...

The Lord's statue.

AS...

She stands BEFORE Him...

As...

She looks up at Him...

(((TALKING TO HIM!!!)))...

As...

She says UNTO HIM...

As...

(She let's Him know)...

"She can't wait for THIS day!",

Though...

(She DON'T know it!)...

THAT...

THIS day, IS the day, He would choose...
(*To make her dreams come true!*)...

And...

All is but perfect.

She...

IS perfect!

Why...

This has GOT TO BE HER!!

And...

IT'S plain for HIM TO SEE...

THAT...

SHE IS THE BADDEST IN THE CITY!!!

And...

The sun is at it's hottest!

AS...

The noon is high!

And...

He's diggin' HER style!

AS...

HE's diggin' her vibe!

'Cause...

She STILL wears her hair CLOSELY shorn!!

And...

(As to why?)...

She keeps her answer short:

"Did anyone ever ask Jesus,
if it hurt,
when they placed on,
the crown of thorns?"

And...

He would NEVER ask!,

'CAUSE...

HE understands!!,...

("She rocks her hair closely shorn like that)...

(((((((BECAUSE SHE FUCKING CAN!!!!!!")))))))...

AND...

Rockin' it rolled-up and cinched -
To just below the bottom,
Of her left knee,
Is the pant leg of her "Free People" -

CRUSHED-VELVET BELL BOTTOM!!!...

And...

Matching her robin's egg nail polish painted toes,
(Exhibited daintly thru her open sandal toes!),
To wear a high-neck - fluted-sleeved - laced-out-blouse -
From "Free People - is what she chose!,
Adorned upon her left wrist,
She wears a Movado,

And...

RIGHT AT HIGH NOON,
Talking to Lord's statue,
Is the ONLY time that,
HER heart's NOT hollow!,

And...

To wear today,
Adorned upon her beautiful nose,
Limited Edition lenses Cazel's of 24 karat gold -
IS what SHE chose!,

And...

Upon seeing all that,
He is PROMPTLY *taken aback!,*
(Back FROM WHAT??),
Back to, thru, and from,
The back of his mind,
OF IMPURE THOUGHTS, OF:
HOW. FIRM. MUST. BE. HER. THIGHS!!,

AND SO...

As...

He's finally reached her,...

As...

(He's standing directly behind her!)...

As...

SHE STILL stands AS STILL,
AS THE LORD'S statue,...

As...

(She still has NO idea!)...

THAT...

TRUE love is about to come true!

And so...

Placed upon the backs of both shoulders,
Are both of his large walnut-sized-knuckled-askewed hands,...

And...

His breath on the back of her neck,
Sends her to the promised land!

And...

Of the gravel...

And...

Of the stones...

She spins 'round quickly,
(Upon all of those!!)...

And...

Upon seeing him,
As she holds her head high,
Now SHE'S the one,
Who's mismerized!,

AND...

(THAT WAS THE LAST THING THAT SHE SAW!!!)...

AS...

He caught and held her fall!

And...

Amongst the gravel...

And...

Amongst the stones...

And...

Amongst the big slabs of concrete,
Formed at their feet,
Formed as toppled-over stalactites and stalagmites,
In formation of the city's plight,
Formed by a bulldozer's blade,
Amongst the Lord's statue that stayed,
He stands there holding dead-weight,
Of a dead-lookin' body,
Of the beauty whom fainted,...

((("DAMN!!! THIS AIN'T-NO-WAY TO GET REACQUAINTED!!!")))...

He says out loud!,...

While...

(Lookin' the FUCK around!!)...

All the while...

WHILE holding her tight,
IN THE MIDDLE OF A FORMER CITY PARK,
UNDER NO LESS THAN,...
HIGH NOON SUNLIGHT!!! (((OY VEY!!!))).

"This ain't no way to be keepin' a LOW profile!,
COPS see me in this fucked up park,
WITH her LIKE THIS IN my arms???,
YOU AIN'T GON' SEE,
THE SUNLIGHT FOR AWHILE!!!",

And...

(Though he's trying not to rough her up),...

BUT...

((("DAMN BABY!!!")))...((("YOU GOTS'TA' WAKE-THA'-FUCK-UP!!!")))

And so...

He rocks her gently in his arms,
Peeping out his whereabouts,
(((OF WHOM MAY BE PEEPING HIM THE FUCK OUT!!!)))...

In case...

It becomes the case,
She fails to be rocked awake,...

And...

HE'S GOT'STA' BE-UP-OUT IN HASTE!!,
(((AIN'T TRYNA' CATCH NO CASE!!!))),

But...

TRUE loves been caught,
For BOTH of them!!,
Ain't gonna leave her behind,
If NEED BE then,
With her in his arms,
(It'll be one hellava' date!),
HE'LL GET THA' FUCK UP OUTTA' THIS PLACE!!!,
IN THE EVENT,
HE'S SEEN WITH,
A DEAD-LOOKING-WOMAN IN HIS ARMS LIKE THIS,
SEEN WITH A MAN AT FIRST GLANCE,
SHE'S NEVER BEEN SEEN WITH BEFORE,
ROCKIN' HER GENTLY,
LIKE HE FELL IN LOVE WITH HER,...
IN THE MORGUE!!!,

And...

Even though,
He's prepared to make their evacuation,
All this time,
SHE'S HAD HIS FULL ATTENTION!!,
Continually continuing the continuance,
Of the gentle rockage,
AND NEVER NOT ONCE DID HE NEVER NOT ONCE,...
Remain fully attentive,
To her current condition.

LOSS

BABY'S LOVE

My baby loves,
My baby loves,
My baby loves,
My baby loves to do me,
My baby loves to do me,
My baby loves to do me wrong.

SCARRED UP FROM THE HEART UP

I'm just scarred up from the heart up,
'Cause I'm that kind of man,
Oh I'm just scarred up from the heart up,
Must be apart of God's plan,
Love don't love me,
And trust don't give a damn,
Hope ran off with faith,
They both took it on the lamb,
Yeah I'm just scarred up from the heart up,
'Cause I'm that kind of man,

These women all have hidden agendas,
Cut me open when they speak of love,
Another scar born across my heart,
When they fly off like the morning dove,
Scar tissue hand-woven all through my heart,
A perfect strain fits it snug like a glove,
Forced to walk the plank again,
Off the Battleship of Love,

I'm just scarred up from the heart up,
'Cause I'm that kind of man,
Oh I'm just scarred up from the heart up,
Must be apart of God's plan,
Love don't love me,
And trust don't give a damn,
Hope ran off with Faith,
They BOTH took it on the lamb!!,
Yeah I'm just scarred up from the heart up,
'Cause I'm that kind of man.

A MILLION MILES AWAY

I've been drinking heavy,
And that's what I'm gonna do,
And when I feel sick,
I'll take another puff or two,
I'm so high I think I'm dying,
Time to crack another brew,
'Cause I've got to get,
A million miles away from you,

And this is some real shit,
I haven't been alive in a year,
But I could fall in love,
From just one kiss from you my dear,
And in a perfect world,
It would just be me and you,
And there'd never be a second,
That you didn't know I loved you,

And when I feel sick,
I take another sip or two,
And when I feel like I'm dying,
I take another puff or two,
But for now, I've got to get,
A million miles away from you,

And I'll never forget that hug,
Or the way you looked at me,
Because I was the luckiest guy in the world,
Because that look was for me,
And you're not feeling me no more,
Is what I think,

So for now, I think,
I'll have another drink,

And when I feel like I'm dying,
I take another puff or two,
And when I feel sick,
I take another sip or two,
And when I think of you,
I know the things I wanna do,
But for now, I got to get,
A million miles away from you,

I'm seeing double,
And my vision is blurry,
I'm at a million miles,
And I'm in no hurry,
And it's killing me to think,
That you don't want me,
But if you ever want me,
A million miles away is where I'll be,

And when I feel sick,
I take another sip or two,
And when I feel like I'm dying,
I take another puff or two,
And the thought you don't want me,
Goes right through,
So for now, I've got to get,
A million miles away from you.

AND SHE DON'T EVEN KNOW MY NAME

You don't want me back,
And I can't get over that,
So I gotta' stay high, baby,
Yeah, I gotta' stay high,

You don't want me no more,
So I got a brand new dirty little whore,
She don't know my name, baby,
Yeah, she don't know my name,

We stay up way past late,
Don't know the last time I ate,
BUT...don't my abs look great, baby?!?,
Yeah, don't my abs look great?,

No SHE DON'T care if I go broke!,
OR if my looks go up in smoke!,
She'll stay with me UNTIL I'm dead!,
That's EXACTLY what she said!,

And she ain't A DAMN THING like you!,
She don't judge me like you USED to!,
I'm her Jack and she's MY Jane!,
And she don't EVEN know my name!,

She picks me up WHEN I'M feeling down!,
ALWAYS knows when to come back around!,
And we DON'T talk about love!,
SHE got me hooked just like a drug!,

I DON'T think about you NO more!,
'CAUSE I got a BRAND NEW dirty little whore!,
So INTO HER I'm going insane!,

And she don't EVEN know my name!,

You don't want me no more,
Had the cops show me the door,
So I gotta stay high, baby,
Yeah, I gotta stay high,

We don't speak of trust,
All we got is lust,
And she don't know my name, baby,
Yeah, she don't know my name,

We stay awake for days,
Gonna put me in the grave,
I think it's fate, baby,
Yeah, I think it's fate,

NO she don't care IF I go broke!,
OR IF my looks go up in smoke!,
SHE'LL stay with me UNTIL I'm dead!,
That's EXACTLY what she said!,

AND she ain't a damn thing LIKE you!,
SHE don't judge me like YOU used to!,
I'm HER Jack and she's my Jane!,
And she don't even know MY name!,

I sniff her up - she holds me down!,
ALWAYS knows when to come back around!,
AND WE DON'T talk about love, 'cause,...
WE DON'T like the way that sounds!!,

I DON'T think about you NO more!,
'CAUSE I got a brand new dirty little whore!,
SO INTO HER I'm going insane!,
AND she don't EVEN know MY name!

IN UR DREAMS

Found love in a strip club,
Found romance in a rehab,
Found affectionate illusions,
Inside the mental institutions,

And...

(THEN there's U!!!)...

Torrid whorin' and horrid!,
BORN TO LIE with ease!!,
SO U can do as U please!!!,

SOOOOOO...

(I'ma let U know)...(HOW DIS'-HERE-SHITZ GOIN' DOWN!)...

Fuck ur kids,
Fuck ur sisters AND brothers,
Fuck ur mom AND fuck ur dad,
AND FUCK UR FAT KNEES!!,

Don't care if u still love me,
Don't care if u act mean,
Bitch, I may not know much,
But I know I'll be in ur dreams,

U'z a lying conniving sneaky bitch,
Walk past wit'a wiggle in your hips,
U say that u don't want me,
Now go throw 'dat ass wit'a switch!,

But I know what it means,
When u play with ur hair and bite ur lip,

Bitch u play too much,
NOW play it off like I don't haunt ur shit!,

Hope ur still alive,
'Cause Heaven AIN'T UR scene!,
Bitch, I may not know much,
But I know I'll be in ur dreams,

U don't want me?,
Oh, the luck!,
Lied to the cops,
Trying to get me locked up!,

Daily dose of vodka and coke,
Shuttin' down ur lungs and guts!,
(AND WHEN I was told that shit),...
(UR PEOPLE thought I'D give a fuck;)

Nope.
No emotion. No love.
Special motherfucker,
U crack me up!,

Bitch ur lost in the sauce,
And in no way as special as u seem,
Bitch, I may not know much,
BUT I KNOW I'll be in UR dreams!!!

WHAT'S TRUST GOT TO DO WITH IT?

I put my whole soul into it,
Would kiss you like it was my last kiss,
When I would lay there looking at you,
I would think is this too good to be true?,

And I would never know when it would go away,
So I would hold you like it was my last day,
And I would kiss you like it was the last time,
'Cause I always wanted you to be mine,

We'd get close, then you'd pull back,
You said you loved me, but it was all an act,
The next girl I won't trust a bit,
But what's trust got to do with it?,

Yeah, I know, next time I'll take it slow,
And I'll just go with the flow,
And love will never come out my mouth,
Its taken me this long to figure this out!,
I'll just do me and get my kicks,...
But what's trust got to do with it?,

My heart felt what it felt,
And my soul saw what it saw,
So the next girl won't get my all,
I'll never open up a door for you,
'Cause that's the shit I used to do,
So if YOU'RE down? - Then WE can kick it!,
BUT trust you girl?? - YOU CAN forget it!!!,

We'd get close, then you'd pull back,

You were never in love with me like that,
The next girl I won't trust a bit,
But what's trust got to do with it?

JET BLACK

You can be bad and be by yourself,
Or be good and be with her,
She wasn't lying,
She meant every word,

The way you been acting and treating her,
Is quite absurd,
Take the pain of not being with her,
It's what you deserve,

You hate her if she moves on,
She'd be smart to do just that,
Get used to your best friends - four walls,
And take comfort in living in black,

'Cause you don't know how to help yourself,
And believe me that's a fact,
Your fate is four best-friend-walls,
And a room that is jet black,

And what's crazier than you,
Is that she still wants you dude,
It's clear to me now,
That her love for me is true,

Makes it seem impossible to believe,
That over and over you doubted that fact,
And so now you sit alone with your best friends,
In a room that is jet black,

And how does her face still light up,
Each time that she sees you?,

It's like her love for you takes the place,
Of all the things you've put her through,

And she don't even feel like,
You're with her anymore,
Like a boat ripped from the dock,
Drifting hopelessly away from shore,

You never expect none - so you don't give none,
And you never cut her any slack,
Just waiting to slip into this coma,
Inside this room that is jet black.

DURING THOSE DAYS

Sabotaged by the world,
I bet you're sick of this,
Sabotoures of the world,
Got in and stayed in,
The ears of your girl,
With a steady hiss,

The sabotoures,
Just had to make sure,
The person you truly are,
She did miss,
Her lips again,
You will never kiss,
I bet it feels to you,
Like The End of Days,
Thee Apocolypse,

Oh, my God!,
I bet you want to break heads!,
Oh, my God!,
I bet you're breakin' your head!,
Oh, my God!,
WHY is God!,
Putting you through this?!?,
Oh, my God!,
I bet you want to beat the brakes!,
Oh, my God!,
I bet you want to cut the heads off the snakes!,
Oh, my God!,
Stayed in the ears of your girl with a steady hiss!,...

AND SO...

During those days,
Have YOU ever wished for death?,
You long to die,
BUT God won't take you yet!,
God HAS witnessed YOUR sins,
Through EVERY SET of eyes you've met!!,

The devil wants your soul,
Through temptation he will lay you to rest,
God WILL strengthen your soul,
And your faith He WILL test,
So God keeps YOU alive,
TO pay off your debt,
And your payment TO God,...
Is your every next breath.

DIE IN YOUR HUG

Why ain't we eatin' the finest of foods?,
And drinkin' the finest of wines?,
Why'd you loosen up your grip, baby?,
Don't you know you were 'sposed to be mine?,

I am the drug you gave up,
And you are the drug I still crave,
I see that look in your eyes, baby,
Like I just walked over your grave,

Why ain't we flyin' 'round the world?,
Why didn't you want to be my girl?,
'Cause not every silver lining has an oyster,
And not every cloud has a pearl,

I gave my soul to you,
Always put you before me too,
And just for you, my baby,
Still ain't nothin' I wouldn't do,

I still feel sick in my gut,
But no matter what,
You're the one I'll always want,
'Til I turn to dust,

You are the one I still love,
And when the end comes,
I still want you to cradle me, baby,
I still want to die in your hug.

CHRISTMAS MOURNING

No it don't look like Christmas morning,
When my baby's not around,
No presents under the tree,
'Cause, no tree to be found,
No snow,
Only tears fall down,
No it don't look like Christmas morning,
When my baby's not around,

No stockings hung up by the fire,
AIN'T NO Christmas lights to take down,
It DON'T EVEN FEEL LIKE it's Christmas,
AIN'T NO MISTLETOE TO BE FOUND!,
NO IT DON'T LOOK LIKE CHRISTMAS MORNING!,
I'm just bending all these strings,
Tryna' DROWN OUT tha' sound,

SITTING by the fire WITHOUT YOU,
IT'S SO COLD!,
I see the flames glowing,
BUT YOUR SHADOW DOESN'T SHOW!,
NAAAAAAH!,
AIN'T NO CHRISTMAS MORNING!,
NO it don't look like Christmas morning,
WHEN MY baby's NOT around,
No snow,
ONLY tears fall down,
YEAH, GO ON AND GIVE IT TO ME ONE MORE TIME!,

No it DON'T feel like Christmas morning,
WHEN THE DEVIL RAT-A-TAT ON THE DOOR,

HE BEEN askin' me,
FOR my whiskey,
HE BEEN beggin' me,
For my soul,

NO IT DON'T LOOK LIKE CHRISTMAS MORNING,
WHEN THE DEVIL RAT-A-TAT ON THE DOOR,
He BEEN ASKIN' me,
FOR whiskey,
HE BEEN beggin' me,
FOR MY SOUL!,
NO IT DON'T LOOK LIKE Christmas morning...

WOUNDED EYES

Crept out from under an undercroft,
For the first time in six weeks,
Headed to a bar he hates,
NOBODY there BETTER DARE to EVEN speak!,
ONLY THERE TO refill his busted heart,

'Cause...

(THE MOTHERFUCKER LEAKS!!!)....

"Hey, barkeep,
give me the STRONGEST shit you got!,
KEEP them comin' straight up,
I DON'T need them on the rocks.,
Just here TO forget ABOUT the shit,
THAT I ALREADY forgot!!",

"Listen, mama,
I DON'T want YOU sittin' next to me!,
You MIGHT be real nice,
but I DON'T want YOUR company!!!",
("Some woman, fucked you up!",
was the barfly's, ONLY reply!),
"Look-here, mama,
I-AIN'T-GOT-NO tears left TO waste!,
ALL I GOT LEFT,
ARE these wounded eyes!!",

And(the barfly, sang):

"WOUND, WOUND, WOUND,...
WOUNDED EYYYYYES!!!,

I SAID, HE GOT,
WOUND, WOUND, WOUND,...
WOUNDED EYYYYYYES!!!",

"Hey, barkeep,
keep them drinks comin' my way.,
And shut the fuck up,
I ain't tryin' to hear what you gotta say.,
Just leave the fucking bottle,
if you want to live another day!",

And(then!)...

He threw that bottle,
At the television screen,
For no other reason than,
HE HATES THAT FUCKING TEAM!!!,
Put his fist through the jukebox,
NOW HE'S FEELING MEAN!!!,
Ripped a line on the bar,...

'CAUSE...

(HE'S A FUCKING FIEND!!!)...

"Save it, barkeep!,
I AIN'T payin' for shit!,
YOU MIGHT think YOU'RE kinda tough,
but YOU DON'T want to get into it!",
("Some woman, fucked YOU over.",
was the barkeep's, ONLY reply!),
"Barkeep, I-ain't-got-no tears left to waste,
All I got left are these wounded eyes.",

AND(THE WHOLE BAR, SANG):

"WOUND, WOUND, WOUND,...
WOUNDED EYYYYYYES!!!
I SAID, HE GOT,
WOUND, WOUND, WOUND,...
WOUNDED EYYYYYYYES!!!".

THE FUCKING YOU GET

Young man,
All these words I say to you,
Is the shit that I've been through,...

If you take a girl out and show her a good time?,
The better your odds of a bump n' grind!,
If you're at the track and your jockey falls?,
It's because Vegas called!,
Nations don't declare war because tempers boil,
It's over a woman, money, or oil,

Young man,
The "Game of Life" is Chess - NOT Checkers,
Best believe,...women play it better!,

Young man,
I'm telling you - it DON'T matter IF you,
Have a fine-ass car - OR IF YOU run to the bitch,
'CAUSE it isn't that far,

Young man,
I'm telling you - it don't matter if you,
Ever felt Heaven in a hug,
OR IF sex got you AND THE bitch - FIENDIN' for it,
Like a drug!,

Young man,
I'm telling you - IT don't matter if you,
Open up a chick's car door,
OR IF the triflin' bitch didn't - have to light-up,
HER cigarettes no more!,

Young man,
I'm telling you - it don't matter if God WAS YOUR witness,
AND WATCHED YOU fall in love,
WITH THAT first kiss!,

Young man,
I'm telling you - it don't matter IF YOU,
HAD a "diaper buddy" - AND HE TELLS YOU,
"You should go WITH ME to this party,
I want to introduce YOU TO a bangin' shorty!,

Young man,
I'm telling you - WHATEVER YOU DO,
DON'T you tell your "diaper buddy",
Of the love, for her, you had,
'Cause NOT-SO-DEEP-down-inside,
IT WILL make him mad!,

Young man,
I'm telling you - KEEP your business - YOUR business,
AND your game tight!,
Bitch-ass house-niggas WILL fuck you,
JUST for spite!,

Young man,
Whatever you "thought" you had - WILL BE anchient history!,
Bitch-ass house-niggas love to,
Turn whores into housewives!,
AND whore-ass housewives,
Love SUPPORTING bitch-ass house-niggas!,
Young man,
That AIN'T NO mystery!,

Young man,

That was years ago,
Spring is for lovers,
It comes and goes,

Young man,
I will never love another,
And I put that on,
The Blessed Mother,

And...

(Then the old man stood up and walked away)...

And...

(HIS parting words stay with ME to this VERY day!)...

As...

(He said to me with no regret)...

"Young man,
There's no need to get upset.,
You CAN'T do shit - ONCE a woman's mind IS set!,
Death and taxes - ARE a sure bet.,
And the fucking you get - AIN'T WORTH the fucking you get!"

PASSION

And so...

He can't see inside the RV,
And it ain't from the lenses of,
His 24 Karat gold tint,

For(You See)...

Inside the RV,...
IT'S dark as shit!,

And...

He's callin' her name,...
"C'mon, Bless!! Quit playin'!!",

Hmm...

(She's probably listening to her OWN songs),...

"If I know my homegirl, Bless?,
SHE'S got on her headphones!",...

And...

"Damn! Where's a light switch,
all up in, this motorhome???",...

And(DAMN!!!)...

(Mixin' those bottles of Dom, on top of them Oxy's,
Is startin' to give his gate, a bit of the wobblies!!),...

As...

(He's still feelin' good!)...

As...

(He's still feelin' on top of the world!!)...

As...

(He's feelin' his way through the dark RV)...

TO...

(Check on his homegirl!)...

And...

"Hmm,...
I guess Bless, is way in the back?,
It's dark-as-fuck in here!,
Eh,...
She's probably just takin' a nap!",

And...

As he reaches for the door,
To the private sleeping quarters,
(way in the back!),
He knocks on it lightly a couple of times,
Before opening it up a slight crack,...

And so...

(While fumbling for the light)...

"Bless, you good?,
I came to make sure my homegirl is alright.",

And...

He opens the door,
While calling her name,

And there's Bless on the floor,
On her back she's just layin',

And...

She's just layin',
To the right of the bed,
30-06 Deer Rifle,
Layin' on the otherside,
Layin' on the floor,
From havin' laid,
That rifle cross the bed,

For(You See!)...

She got down on her knees,
Beside the bed like she was prayin',...

(I DOUBT that she was!)

But...

(I swear to God)...(I PRAY THAT SHE WAS PRAYIN'!!!)

For(YOU SEE!!)...

Bless, laid her body cross the bed,
Cocked a custom Fedora hard to the side,
On top of her head,
At the tip of that 30-06 barrel,
She placed her forehead,
She struggled and strained,
With the passion of a lover,
And once she reached that trigger,
She pulled that motherfucker!,

(DON'T NOTHIN' KICK LIKE THAT!!!)

(It must have made a horrible sound)...

When...

That deer rifle went off,
Sending through her head,
A 30-06 round!,
Blood.

All different sizes and shapes of her brain.

Teeth.

Skull-the-fuck-fragments.

And...

(Most of her face!)

Was simply blown,
All-the-fuck-over the place!!!!!,

(It was all-the-fuck-over,
TOLD him she was sick of this shit,
She just wanted it over),...

"Is that skull??,
Holy shit!!,
I think that is skull!!",
The ceiling of the private sleeping quarters,
He looks up and sees up above!!,

Too many, some bloody,
Some white, all jagged,
From all different shapes and sizes,
Of Bless' skull fragments!!,

Big clumps of brain everywhere,

And the more he stood there and looked,
The more he became aware,
Of the floor, of the walls,
Of the ceiling, of that big pool of blood,
Under the bed, gettin' gummy and elastic,
From all that blood, that drained THROUGH the mattress!,

Of the more he inspected,
STILL pooling and forming,
Of the drainage,
Under the bed it collected,

And she was only 16,
Laying there in the all red,
EVERYTHANG,
With everythang red,

On her back,
What a sight,
30-06 round went,
Through her head,
And clear outta sight,

It peeled off everythang,
From the top of her right,
Cheekbone, on up,
(And I give her credit for her guts!),

Bless took control of her life,
By controlling when she'd be dead,
Peeled her fucking face off,
(Ever see a 16 year old female,
Laying there like that?,
Missing her face and her head??),...

(You have now!)...(Welcome to "SYKE World"!!!)...

And she was only 16,
And he says to himself and Bless,
"They can't take you away from me, homegirl.",

For(You See)...

'Cept for what was left,
Of her right cheekbone,
From her bottom lip, on up,
THAT SHIT was gone!,

For(You See!)...

Bless, took a hardline,
And was left with a hardline cut,
Of partial facial bones,
Beneath where her right eye socket was!,

WHICH...

(Was only WHAT was left,
OF her facial flesh!),...

AND(IN ADDITION TO THAT!!!)...

Long n' Curly Hair of Mermaid,
Is what she had,
She had brain sniglets,
All-up-in it,
Just above the back of her neck,
Of what she had left!!!,

And...

(Try not to cry)...

AS...

He knelt down next to her,
Removing the 24 Karat gold lenses,
From his eyes,...

For(You See!)...

When he removed her Mermaid Hair,
From what was left of her face,
THAT'S when he was met with,
Inner peace and grace,

For...

(Before his eyes turned wet?)...

He found that he,
Was looking directly,
Into the ONLY eye,
THAT Bless had left!,

Oh(Yeah!)...

(Of, not to cry?)...(DO YOUR BEST!)

Nah...

(It's alright now)...(GO ON AND CRY!!!)

AS...

A mix of blood and tears,
Came from his eyes!!,
Fresh weepings of blood,
Streamed down his face,

And...

(Of, her face?)...

Well...

He never did see it.

But...

(Its gotta be SOMEWHERE,
'Round this place!!!),...

FOR(YOU SEE!!!)...

From that jagged cheekbone on down,
Of what was left of her head,
What a hollowed-out-mess!!!,

And...

Laying there like that,...
Was his homegirl, Bless.

ALL-RED-EVERYTHANG-MINEFIELD-ROOM!!!

And so...

(Under murderous and eyes of alibis)...

I present YOU with a dare!

To...

Come enter the room with him.

For...

HE wants YOU to see,
What he saw for himself,
But didn't see,
'Cause it wasn't there,
And he wants YOU to see for YOURSELF,
What YOU won't be able to see,
'Cause it won't be there,
For YOU to see either!,

(Make sense?)

Well...

GO AHEAD then! AND enter THAT room!

(((If YOU dare!!!)))

AND...

Take a look WITH him,
For YOURSELF!!!,
And LET him show YOU,
What HE SAW,

What WASN'T there,
And SEE if YOU can see,
What you can't see,
FOR yourself!!!,

And(As YOU do!)...

Follow him,
Into THAT room,
He's gonna WARN you,
(And three others too!!!),
As to what,
YOU'RE gonna HAVE to do!,

And...

(Since YOU'RE still reading,...I give YOU credit FOR YOUR guts!!)...

AND SO...

WITH warning heeded,
As all of you proceeded,
Is that what you NEEDED,
(To do AS YOU go!),
YOU'RE GONNA' damn-near,
HAVE to TIPTOE,
Into, through, and around,
This - ALL-RED-EVERYTHANG -
MINEFIELD-ROOM!!!,

(JUST to get to Bless' SIDE of the bed!)

Brain sniglets in clumps.
Of varying shapes and sizes.
Blood.
Teeth.

And...flesh chunks!!

(Will be ALL OVER this - ALL-RED-EVERYTHANG-MINEFIELD-FLOOR!!!)

BUT...

(Don't YOU forget to ALWAYS LOOK UP!!!)

'Cause...

(There's a whole lot more!)

'Cause...

(ALL THAT SHIT is ON the ceiling too!!)

And...

If YOU ain't payin' attention,
WHEN some of that shit breaks free,
(and comes down!),
Well, then, it's GONNA' be YOU!,
NOW YOU'RE the one,
With the FACE-FLESH-CHUNKS!!!,
AND WITH THE BRAIN SNIGLETS!!!,
(ALL UP in YOUR hair!!!),
AND DOWN the BACK of YOUR NECK!!!,
AND ON top of YOUR head!!,

But...

(WHATEVER you do,...WATCHOUT for the brain sniglets!!)

And...

(If you don't know what YOU should be looking for?)...

Well...

(HAVE NO FEAR!!!)

For...

(That triflin' motherfucker got you!)...(With ANOTHER warning!)...

They're kinda pink or kinda gray.
Might kinda be red from blood.
(And THIS next part of the warning,
SHOULD make YOU happy!),
They might kinda remind you of your childhood!, (Awww!),...

'CAUSE...

Brain sniglets ALSO kinda look like TAFFY!!!

And...

WHATEVER YOU do,
DON'T STEP ON them!!,
OR get them ON your clothes!!,
(Worse than dog shit!!!),
YOU'LL have a hell of a time,
Diggin' them out,
the bottom tread,
STUCK all-up-in,
YOUR shoe's soles!,

'Cause...

Brain sniglets are ALSO kinda STICKY and TACKY!!!

AND ALL THAT is what,
YOU'LL be SOOOOOO TUNNEL-VISIONED on!,
As YOU TIPTOE through THAT room!,
As YOU follow THAT triflin' motherfucker,
Into, around, and through,

(In painstaking-avoidance!),
OF the teeth.
OF the sniglets.
OF the blood.
OF the chunks.
AND the lumps!

And(Lest we forget!)...

YOU AIN'T gonna be able TO avoid...THE SMELL!!!

'CAUSE...

(((THAT'S SOME SHIT YOU WON'T EVER FORGET!!!)))

BUT, WAIT!!!,
THEN it's gonna hit YOU!!!!!!,
THE very reason WHY,
YOU ARE IN THE ROOM,
The reason in the first place,
You DARED to,
Follow THAT triflin' motherfucker into!,

And(ALL this time!)...

(YOU'RE DEALING WITH ALL THIS SHIT!!!)...

Trying YOUR best,
NOT TO STEP,
On the...brain sniglets!
Or on the massive blood loss.
As YOU tiptoe around facial flesh.

(Shiii!t, YOU'RE even trying to avoid the teeth!)(And stuff that kinda looks like meat!)

And...

(WITH ALL THIS SHIT IN YOUR HEAD)...

When you see her,
You're like, "Oh yeah,...
there's a girl laying here dead."

(And THAT'S the most fucked up part of it all)

As...

Having met the dare,
(And heeded the warnings!!),
Hanging back from the body a bit,
Are YOU and the rest,

AS...

THAT triflin' motherfucker,
The only one to dare go closer,
He's once again,
Back with his homegirl, Bless!,

And so...

After confirming,
What he knew,
What he saw,
That he didn't see,
('CAUSE, it wasn't there!),
Oh, lucky YOU!,
THAT triflin' motherfucker,...
Wants to begin WITH YOU!,

For(YOU SEE)...

(He thinks YOU just might be sharper than the other three!!!)

AND SO...

(He starts WITH YOU SPECIFICALLY!!!)...

To see if YOU CAN SEE,
WHAT he COULDN'T see!,
('CAUSE, it WASN'T there!),

But(FIRST!)...

The MOST triflin',
WANTS for YOU,
To THINK about WHAT'S missin'!...

(And of what's missing?)...

DON'T YOU DARE, SAY:
"YEAH!!!,...
HER MOTHERFUCKIN'-FACE!!!",

(Naaaaaah!)

So crane YOUR neck!
And DO inspect!
There's NO tear tracks!
NOT a trace!

Which means...

She had gotten to,
HER point in life,
Where SHE wanted to,
TAKE her OWN life!

(Right here)...(And right now)

For(YOU see!)...

THAT triflin' motherfucker,
DON'T KNOW if she knew,

(or even cared!),
Of what she was about to do,
To her face!,...

BUT(WHAT HE DOES KNOW IS)...

She WANTED TO leave this world.
Right here. And right now.
And did so...without a tear.
Not one trace.

WRIST WATCH
(AUTOPSY ASSISTANT - PRELUDE)

By following the smell of formaldehyde,
You're already inside,
WITH THAT STENCH OF,
Deterioration AND decay,

And you're in there,
Like most folks - LIKE THESE folks -
(That TOOK for granted - THAT NIGHT is guaranteed - dammit!) -
WHEN putting on in the morn,
The underwear they're STILL wearing,

And you're inside with,
Deterioration's STENCH,
And with ALL THOSE dead people,
IN a state of decay,

And you're inside with,
ALL THOSE DEAD PEOPLE,
STILL with their watch on their wrist,
That - that morning - when they did it - didn't,
Know that they'd be dead,...later that day.

AUTOPSY ASSISTANT

And so...

Come break into a morgue,
With these four,
Well, really five,
But she's already died,

BUT...

(YOU'LL need to carefully listen!)...

AS...

The One that goes by "The MOST Triflin'",
TO SOME shit - hips them,

AS...

(A lesson - to YOU - AND THEM - HE gives!!!)...

For...

YOU WILL need to put on this white garment,
(And I don't mean to be an alarmist!),

BUT...

YOU WILL need to blend!,
(OR the authorities they will send!),

For...

YOU WILL look JUST LIKE an imposter doctor,
Once YOU HAVE on your "Medical Examiner's" lab coat!,

WELL...

(AT LEAST - for YOUR SAKE - I hope!!!)...

But...

(Then again,...AIN'T NONE OF 'EM DOCTORS!!!!)...

But...

(YOU'RE in luck!!)...

'CAUSE...

(It's ONLY proper!)...

FOR the triflin' one that HAS done this before,
TO GIVE ALL Y'ALL just a lil' sumfin'-sumfin' TO reassure,...

AS...

(YOU,...AND THEM,...reach the door of the morgue!!!!!)...

"As you can see,
the door to the morgue,
looks like just any other.

Ain't nuthin' special to it...

It looks just like an unassuming door,
on the front of an unassuming house,
next to some shutters."

BUT...

"There's just SOMETHIN' 'BOUT,
that lil' black plastic sign,
with "MORGUE" engraved,
in white recessed lettering,
THAT MAKES people shudder!"

For(YOU See!)...

"Ain't NOBODY in this entire hospital dyin',
TO GET in THIS door AND on that I AIN'T lyin'!"

AND...

"THAT'S what separates THIS DOOR FROM all the others!!"

And so...

("The One", in the know)...

Knowing - HE'LL have - "enough" - "uninterrupted-time" -
TO DO - what-the-fuck HE came there - TO DO,
Once again,..."The MOST Triflin' One",...gains entry,...

But...

"Reader" BEWARE!!!

And(yes)...

(((That means YOU!!!)))

For(You See)...

IF...

(YOU AIN'T used to this life?)...

IF...

(YOU'RE...NEW to THIS life??)...

Well...
((((((REASONS for YOU to SHUDDER ARE plenty!!!!!!))))))

FOR...

Once, Bless gets wheeled in,
For once, they are all inside,

That triflin'-imposter-doctor closes and locks,
THAT DOOR to the hospital's morgue,
LOCKING ALL Y'ALL INSIDE!!!!!!,

And(THEN)...

(HE...turns on some lights!)...

AND...

(To the others' surprise!)...

Finding themselves,
Standing in a small office,...
IS ALL THAT they find!,

(Followed by the relief)...(OF a BIG COLLECTIVE-SIGH!!!)))

As(they!)...(And YOU!)...(Feel that elephant step)...(From off of their chests!!!!)...

AND(THEN)...(That elephant)...(RIGHT back on it steps!!!!)...

AS(they!)...(And YOU!!)...

WATCH the experienced-imposter-doctor,
Walk towards ANOTHER door,
That is BEING partially obscured,
By some tall filing cabinets,
NEXT TO a small wooden desk!,

For...

(Just on the otherside)...(of that OTHER door)...

Well...

THAT'S WHERE the smell freezes and hangs!

(((Your mettle it will test!!!)))

For...

JUST THROUGH this small office...IS the hospital's sarcophagus!

And...

(OH YEAH!!!)...(Hey, Reader!)...(Of THAT smell?)...(THAT, freezes and hangs??)

Well...

(YOU CAN TRY to shower THAT shit off!)...(oh)...(you can TRY!!)...

And...

(When you TRY?)...(DO TRY)...(to do YOUR best!)...

FOR(YOU SEE!!!)...

THAT distinct smell of the morgue,
LOVES TO marry mucus membranes,
'Til death does its part -
Forever STUCK -
To all of yours!,

However...

DON'T be scary!!!,
(((HOW BAD DO YOU WANT IT???))),
THAT'S just the SMELL,
Of the DEAD BODIES at rest!!!,

(Psst!)...(Hey, Reader!)...(JUST put on that stiff upper lip)...

AND...

DO try,

And act like,
You AIN'T posin'!,

For...

IT'S JUST chemicals and shit.
Hangin'.
FROZEN!!!

(FROZEN INSIDE THAT "atmosphere" of a COOLER!!!)

But...

Even that DON'T COMPARE to when,
The Medical Examiner's assistant,
(WITH PRECISION),
Hits that decedent WITH a "Y" incision!,
(((Opening up that "perMEATion"!!!))),
OF the decedent's LAST SUPPER and shots!,
Of some dead motherfucker,
That GOT SHOT DEAD from some shooter!,
Hangin'.
FROZEN!!!
IN that "atmosphere" of a cooler!,

'CAUSE...

(((THAT'S some nasty-ass SMELLIN' shit!!!)))

So...

TRY as you might!

BUT...

ALL the alcohol, drugs and shots,
YOU'LL NEED TO DO,

TO FORGET that shit???,

Well...

IT AIN'T GONNA' WORK!!!

For...

((((((NONE of that shit can make YOU forget!!!!!!))))))

(OH!)...(you CAN wash it out YOUR clothes!)...

HOWEVER...

IT AIN'T gon' wash away,
THAT smell out of YOUR...mucus membranes!,

FOR...

((((((THAT SHIT - GON' FOREVER REMAIN - THE-FUCK-UP YOUR nose!!!))))))

AND SO...

FOR YOU, "The Reader",
For YOU, I have a SAFE BET,
THAT "skulldust sawdust"
Momentarily to be kickin' up,...

When that imposter doctor starts diggin',
An oscillating autopsy saw,
Deep-down-and-grindin'-away,
IN a dead motherfucker's SKULL!,

Well...

THAT SHIT WILL BE stuck,
Up in YOUR mucus membranes!,
(WELCOME TO "SYKE WORLD"),

(((YOUR LIFE WILL NEVER BE THE SAME!!!))).

For...

THAT'S SOME SHIT -
YOU AIN'T NEVER -
(((EVER!!!))) -
GON' BE ABLE -
TO LIVE WITHOUT!!!,

FOR(YOU SEE!!!)...(Psst!)...(Hey, Reader!)...

(((That SMELL is embedded IN that "SKULLDUST-SAWDUST"!!!)))

AAAAAAND...

THAT SHIT WILL BE embedded,
IN YOUR mucus membranes,
That lines the insides,
OF YOUR FUCKIN' SNOUT!!,

And(Oh yeah)...(HEY, READER!!!!!!)...(ABOUT that smell??)...

Well...

(DON'T YOU EVER - EVER - have NO doubt ABOUT it!)...

'Cause...

NOT EVEN hard liquor,
(can OR will!),
Make that smell,
Leave YOUR mind!,

(Psst!)...(Hey, Reader!)...(HA!)...

(((YOU WILL NEVER - EVER - LIVE WITHOUT IT!!!)))

FOR(YOU SEE!!!)...

It's JUST LIKE after,
Chapter after "SYKE WRLD" Chapter,
YOU can trust,
THAT ALL THIS "Skulldust Sawdust",
WILL stay with YOU,...
'Til the end of time!,

So...

Are YOU ready to delve?

Or...

Are YOU gonna take a dive?

Or...

Are YOU ready to read some shit - I bet - YOU'LL never forget!?!

(It's alright, go on and take your time)...

Psst...

Hey, reader,...LOOKATCHA'!!!

YOU KEPT ON READING!!!...(didn't YOU!?!)...

(EVEN AFTER THAT SAFE BET!!!)

Alright, let's get into it...

And so...

AS YOU WATCH that triflin'-imposter-doctor,
DOIN' what he came there TO DO,
((Now elbow deep!!)),
Triggers get triggered,
INTO YOUR MIND,...triggers WILL creep,...

Under the grinding-sound,
Of that oscillating saw,
That saw blade moves,
Side-to-side,
Fast as the wings of a hummingbird's beat!!,

Under memories,
Of the mind,
Of consciousness,
Under subconsciousness,
Under the mind,
Under a hummingbird's beat,
Into the mind,
It's beginning to creep,
Side-to-side,
Left-to-right,
Right-to-left,
It has crept,
Side-to-side,
Right-to-left,

Triggered-mutterings,
Of triggers get-muttered,
Under breath,
Side-to-side,
"The destruction of it all.",
Right-to-left,

"It's just...that surgical shit.",
"THAT, "Y" INCISION SHIT!!!",
"THAT PRECISION SHIT",
(((Horrific-triggers getting tripped!!!))),
"OF SKIN getting split!!!",

(Psst!)...(Hey, reader)...(guess what???)...

THAT'S THE ROOM YOU'RE IN!,
YES YOU!!!,
RIGHT NOW!!!,
YOU ARE IN that autopsy ROOM!!,
(I SEE YOU!!!),
AND YOU SEE YOURSELF THERE TOO!!,
AND AT THIS MOMENT OF TRUTH,
I'LL PROVE IT TO YOU!!!,

For...

A subconscious-reaction,
ALREADY happened,
When YOU breathed IN all those,
Fine sawdust-like-fragments of skull,

(Need MORE PROOF???)

(Hold on tight, as I make you CONSCIOUSLY-AWARE!!!)...

For...

That "tingling-sensation",
YOU ARE ABOUT TO start feeling,...
Tingling IN the bridge of YOUR nose!,
THAT'S from WHEN YOU breathed in,
All that skulldust-sawdust!,

And...

The reason being,
YOU CAN NOW FEEL THAT TINGLING,
Growing stronger NOW,
Is because,...

THAT SKULLDUST-SAWDUST,
Has been EATING AWAY,
At your mucus membranes,
THIS ENTIRE TIME,
After all!,

And you wanna know WHY,
YOU CAN FEEL all that,
microscopic-skulldust EATING AWAY AT,
YOUR NOSE???,

(oh shit...HERE IT COMES!!!)...

'CAUSE...

Skulldust-Sawdust,
LOOKS A WHOLE LOT LIKE -
dust mites -
When you get up close!,

(AND THAT'S THE SHIT YOU JUST BREATHED UP YOUR NOSE!!!)

AND...

ALL OF THOSE AIRBORNE-DUST-MITES AIN'T COMIN' BACK DOWN!!!

And...

I-KNOW-YOU-KNOW,
YOU can feel ALL of those,
airborne-skulldust-dust-mites,

'Cause...

YOU CAN JUST PICTURE,

ALL those skulldust-dust-mites,
UP IN YOUR NOSE RIGHT NOW!!!,

AND...

(THAT'S WHY YOU CAN FEEL THAT SHIT TINGLING!!!)

Welcome to "SYKE WRLD"!

(OH, YOU'RE IN IT NOW!!! SO, DON'T TURN BACK NOW!!!)

For...

There's work to be done!

(Dirty work!)

After all...

Don't YOU WANT TO SEE if you are able,
To handle all of that is about to happen,
ON THAT silver stainless-steel autopsy table???,

For...

(If you turn back now?)...(YOU'RE leaving too soon!!)

AFTER ALL...

Don't YOU WANT TO HEAR the gurgle??,
Don't YOU WANT TO SMELL,
What's GONNA' run down,
That floor-drain in the - MIDDLE - of that room???,

(Well, I SEE YOU stuck around!)

'CAUSE...

Ain't that YOU covered in Skulldust Lice?,
Can't YOU SEE that dead guy lying,

There on his back,
Face still with the look of pain,
On top of THAT,
Autopsy table EQUIPPED,
WITH HOSES AND DRAINS!?!,

Can't YOU JUST IMAGINE,
What IT MUST be like,
With NOTHIN' but a white towel,
Covering YOUR privates,
AS YOU lay there NAKED ,
And COLD as ice?!?,

Can't YOU SEE that GRAY postmortem skin??,
And how AT UNNATURAL ANGLES,
HIS knees and elbows are BENT!?!,
(Can't YOU SEE that this IS FROM,
The RIGOR MORTIS that HAS set in?!?),

Can't YOU SEE it would be ONLY right,
YOU can't just watch,
YOU GOTTA HELP that triflin'-imposter-doc,
To FORCE those JOINTS,
Back in the OPPOSITE direction,
TO BREAK that rigor mortis, RIGHT???,

After all...

Can't YOU SEE that orange block of rubber??,
UPON WHICH,...
The BACK of that dead dude's head is at rest,

(NASTY SOUND!!!)...

As...

The rigor GETS SNAPPED IN HIS NECK,

AS...

His CHIN gets buried in his CHEST!!!

And...

Can't YOU SEE that triflin-imposter-doctor,
With scalpel in hand,
'Bout to give a deep long slice?!?,

As...

(Starting in the back of that dead dude's head!)...

That triflin'-imposter-doctor drags that blade IN the skin!

AS...

((THOSE OPEN DEAD EYES say unto YOU!!)),...
"I WANT TO DIE, ALL OVER AGAIN!!!"

And...(Ain't that YOU??)...

AIN'T THOSE...YOUR EYES,
Following that scalpel blade,
RIGHT NOW AS IT SLICES,
Around the ENTIRE circumference,
OF HIS head???,

And...(Ain't YOU THE ONE??)...

That...(Just VOMITED IN THE BACK OF YOUR MOUTH???)...

At...(THE EASE, of the way)...

That RAZOR-sharp scalpel blade,
SPLIT-OPEN-WIDE,

THAT GRAY FOREHEAD!?!,

But...(You're not alone!)...

'Cause...(YOU'RE being followed!!)...

For(YOU SEE!!)...

FOLLOWED BY that scalpel blade,...
Is THE FLOW,...
Of the DANK DARK BLOOD OF THE DEAD!!!,

And...(((LEST WE FORGET!!!!!!)))...

WATCHING along in there WITH YOU,
(In that: skulldust-sawdust-airborne-dust-mite-cooler-of-a-room!),
YOU'RE BEING WATCHED - BY THE SPIRITS - OF THE DEAD!!!!!!,

And...

AS YOU ARE BEING WATCHED,
All this time,
YOU'VE BEEN WATCHING ALONG,
With all FOUR of them!!!!,

For...

ALL this time,
IT'S BEEN YOU,
(Right in there WITH the rest of them!),
THAT BROKE INTO THAT COOLER OF A ROOM!!!,

And...

(RIGHT ABOUT NOW!)...

I'D BET IN A SECOND,

YOU COULD USE A SHOWER!!,

As...

UPON YOU,
Countless microscopic,
skulldust-sawdust-dust-mites HAVE landed!,

And...

UPON YOU,
They HAVE BEGUN to devour!!!!!!,

For...

(IN THAT ROOM)...

YOU ARE BEGINNING TO GET covered!

(TAKE A LOOK ALL AROUND YOU!!!)

Can't YOU SEE THEM,
In that microscopic cloud,
AS they hover???,

(And here's a lil' hint)...

ON YOUR CLOTHES,
They may look like LINT!,

(BUT they're even smaller!)...

'CAUSE...

YOU'RE STILL BREATHING THAT SHIT IN!!!

(And, I'ma let you in on a secret!)...(Though, I hate, and ain't, a snitch!)

BUT...

YOU'RE GONNA' hate yourself,

WHEN YOU feel yourself,
FINALLY giving in!,

(And, you're probably gonna be on some - "How'd he know this SHIT?!?")

(And AT YOURSELF, YOU WILL GET pissed!)...

WHEN...

YOU HEAR yourself, saying, "Now, AIN'T THIS a bitch!"

When...

YOU FEEL that YOU COULD NO LONGER,
Fight the URGE,
To SCRATCH YOUR HEAD and,
That, YOU COULD NO LONGER RESIST!!!,

'Cause...

(skulldust-dust-mites MAKE YOUR SCALP ITCH!!!!!!)

(And YOU WILL be thinking it!)...

EVEN IF,
YOU don't say it aloud,
"HOW'D HE KNOW,
I'M gonna fight the urge,
to fingersweep out my ear?!?",

(Well?)...(I'll fucking tell you!)...

'CAUSE...

There's one or two of them lil' fuckers -
RIGHT-THA'-FUCK-NOW -
That got all the way down,...
IN YOUR EAR CANAL!!,

And...

(I bet YOU didn't even realize)

But...

YOU WILL!

WHEN...

(YOU catch yourself sniffin'!)

'CAUSE...

YOU'RE BEGINNING TO get,
The SMELL OF DANK,
Dead blood ON YOUR SKIN!!!,

And...

Ain't that YOU,
That's ABOUT TO FEEL,
Go through YOUR body,
A DEATH-COLD CHILL?!?,

WHEN...

YOU REALIZE,
THERE'S TOOOOOO MUCH DETAIL,
FOR THIS FUCKING POEM,
TO NOT BE REAL!!!,

So...

(There ain't no use in YOU screamin'!)

YOU IN THAT ROOM,
WITH dank dark dead blood...
AS IT'S STREAMIN'!!!,

So...

HOW DO YOU FEEL,
BEING IN THAT ROOM,
AS THAT STENCH,
BEGINS TO HANG IN THE AIR FREEZIN'!?!?!?!,

(And, to that sick-imposter-doctor, ain't that dead man bound!?)

As...

(Starting at the temples)

YOU WATCH,
That sick-fuckin'-doc,
Perform TWO LONG SLICES DOWN!!,

As...

(All this time)...

YOU'VE BEEN IN IT WITH HIM!!

As...

YOU get SICKENED BY THE IMAGE,
OF THE CONTRAST,
OF the graying,
OF the gaping,
OF that dark dank dead blood,
OF those two long cuts,
(Starting at the temples!!),
SPLIT in the skin!!,

(After, and then)...

That sick-triflin'-imposter-doctor-morgue-breakin'-in,
A helping hand TO HIM,...YOU LEND,...

As...

YOU...assist him!

As...

YOU NOW KNOW,
IT'S NOW ON YOU!!!

(To lend a helping hand!)...

There's SOOOOOO much blood!

And...

IT'S COMING OUT THICK!

AND...

YOU KNOW NOW,...
YOU GOTTA' DO SOMETHIN'!!!

(THIS ain't no TIME FOR YOU TO BE gettin' SICK!)

So...

DO WHAT YOU CAN,
To keep them -
Hot-nasty-bitter-TASTING-stomach-biles -
DOWN SOUTH!
YOU don't WANT TO TASTE THAT SHIT again,
IN the back of YOUR MOUTH!!!,

So...

(IN YOU),

YOU FIND THE STRENGTH!!!

As...

YOU BEGIN...

To wipe and rinse!

(That dead man's blood, YOU BEGIN to wash away!)

As...
IT'S streakin' down BOTH SIDES,
Of his DEAD-GRAY FACE!!

(If YOU WOULD SEE that LOOK IN YOUR EYES RIGHT NOW)...

Then...

YOU WOULD SEE LOVE!!!

'Cause...

That sick-ass-imposter-doctor,
HAS NOW GOTTEN INTO YOUR MIND!

And...

(YOU don't even REALIZE)...

That...

(YOU ARE NOW SEEING things,...
Differently IN TIME!)...

FOR...

YOU NOW HAVE BEGUN,
TO THINK fondly upon,
All THAT dank-smellin' DARK streaks of blood!,
(CONTRASTED upon a canvas of gray!),

'CAUSE...

There ain't no life,
IN that dead man's face!

(OH, YOU'RE IN IT NOW!)

So...

(HERE COMES the REALLY fucked up part!)...

AS...

(YOU REALIZE)...

THAT...

(YOU ARE BEGINNING TO SEE,
Those streaks of blood as art!)...

AND...

Because of that,
OF yourself,
YOU BEGIN TO FEEL disgrace!,

As...

(YOU NOW BEGIN TO SEE ALL THAT BLOOD...as finger paint!!!)...

So...

GO AHEAD!

(DON'T BE SCARY!)...

FEEL THAT cold-wet-dead-skin in YOUR bare hands!!

As...

YOU ASSIST that sick-ass-imposter-doc,

Ever so Triflin',
AFTER HE GAVE BOTH sides,
(OF THAT dead motherfucker's head),
TWO LONG DEEP SLICES!!,
AFTER YOU WATCHED,
That triflin'-sick-imposter-doc,
Take THAT scalpel,
And SPLIT THE SKIN,
(Of that dead motherfucker's head),
ALL THE WAY AROUND!!!!!!,
WITH A nice tight grip,
Of cold wet dead skin,
YOU give a GOOD TUG,
AS YOU HELP him,
PULLING the dead's FACE,
RIGHT ON DOWN!!!,

(YOUR stomach is gettin' a bit jacked NOW, ain't it?)...

AND...

YOU'RE feeling a bit dizzy,
And lightheaded,
OF YOUR ACTS,
SO HEINOUS!!!,

(Can't YOU JUST IMAGINE THE TASTE???)...

Of that DANK DARK DEAD BLOOD,
AS IT gurgles down that autopsy room's,
Floor grate of center drainage!,

And...(oh yeah)...(HEY, READER!)...(YOU CAN wear a mask!)...

And...(I give you credit, for YOUR guts!)...

'Cause...

(YOU are STILL READING!!!)...

For...

YOU MUST BE up for the task!

(YOU, triflin' mutha' fucka', YOU!!!!!!)

HOWEVER...

(Even WITH a mask!)...

If YOU'RE STILL GETTIN' A HINT,
OF THAT STENCH,...guess what??

(OH, AND YOU, BEST BELIEVE!!!)...

SOME of that microscopic "skulldust-sawdust",
WILL FOREVER get stuck,
(TO YOUR mucus membranes!),
AS YOU BREATHE!!!,

For...

'Round that mask OF YOURS,
It WILL FIND its way 'round!,
Kicked-up from,
That autopsy saw!,
MAKING that AWFUL,
WOODSHOP SOUND!!!,

And...

(THAT'S what YOU ARE breathing in!)...

And...

(Now ain't THIS A bitch!?)...

'Cause...

STILL eatin' away AT YOUR SCALP,
ARE YOUR tiny-skulldust-dust-mite FRIENDS!,

And...(Psst!)...(hey, reader)...(I KNOW WHAT YOU'RE THINKING!)...

"THIS MOTHERFUCKER, ACTUALLY GOT MY SCALP ITCHING!!!"

(GO ON AND ADMIT IT!)

'CAUSE...

YOU KNOW THAT'S WHAT YOU'RE THINKING!

AND...(YOU'RE THINKING)...

"THIS MOTHERFUCKER, BETTER NOT REMIND ME, OF THE BRIDGE OF MY NOSE AGAIN!!"

'CAUSE...

THEN YOU WILL START TO GET THE INKLING,
THAT I CAN ACTUALLY FEEL,
THE BRIDGE OF MY NOSE...TINGLING!!!,

(((I told y'all THIS POEM WILL TAKEOVER your brain!!!)))

And...

(YOU didn't even realize it but)...

YOUR FACE AROUND YOUR NOSE,...
Just started itching again!,

For...

THEY'RE STILL ALL UP IN YOUR NOSE,
RIGHT NOW!!!,
THAT'S WHERE ALL of those -
"tiny-sawdust-like-skull-fragments-of-the-DEAD" -
WILL BE FOUND!!!,

Kicked-up and breathed in,
(As that AWFUL WOODSHOP SOUND IS being made!),
Kicked-up and breathed in,
BY A quick-as-shit-HALF-MOON-thin-lookin' blade!,

MOVIN' side-to-side!,
Left-BACK-TO-right!,
Such a DANGEROUS-COMBINATION!!!,
(That saw and that sick-imposter-doctor-the-MOST-trife!!),

For...

They both got precision and speed!!

(Psst!)...(HEY, reader!)...

(((YOU BEST WATCH YOURSELF 'round that imposter-doctor-the-MOST-trife!)))

FOR...

THAT BLADE IS FASTER THAN,
A hummingbird's wings can beat!!

(Psst!)...(HEY, READER!!!)...

(Stay at a safe distance WHEN YOU SEE that imposter-doctor-the-MOST-trife!!!)...

He got that oscillating autopsy saw of bone and meat.

'Cause...("DAAAAAAYYUUUUM!!!")...

"THAT IMPOSTER-DOCTOR IS SOOOOOO-DAMN-TRIFE!!!, WHAT-THA'-FUCK is he doin' NOW??, GRIPPIN' UP,...supplies???",

"What's he GONNA' DO with that BIG RED SPOOL of thread??"

("Oh shit!)...(Combined WITH)...(that BIG-hooked-sewing-needle SO THICK!!!")...

"That imposter-doc GOT TO HAVE SOME PLANS COOKED-UP in his head!"

And...("OH, GOOD LORD!!!")...

"Is he REALLY gonna take THAT AUTOPSY SAW??"

And...("WHATS'HE NEED")...

"Those viles WITH the RED, PURPLE, and GRAY rubber-topped-stoppers for???"

For...

(FROM the gore - THOSE WERE ONLY THOUGHTS - FROM the four!!!!)...

For(YOU SEE!!)...

(Nobody chimed in!!!)...

FOR...(RIGHT ABOUT NOW!!!)...(I'd EVEN bet!)...

(That YOU have - YOUR OWN - stiff upper lip!)...

(Of YOUR: "While-I'M-in-this-morgue-Self-Defense!")...

With dead bodies zipped-up on gurneys to the left,
With dead bodies zipped-up on gurneys to his right,
With one poor-wet-cold-dead-blue-motherfucker,
(Left layin' there!), DEAD NAKED!,
With a whole lotta other dead-motherfuckers,
Behind those silver stainless heavy-handled doors,
WHERE other dead-motherfuckers,
FEET FIRST,
Were SLID inside!!,

AND(THEN)...

(((YOU GOT THE FREEZER!!!)))

(Come!)...(YOU'LL WANT TO have a LOOK AT THIS!)...

FULLY STOCKED,
WITH (AND OF!),
Compound fractures and overdoses!!,
ENCASED WITHIN their zippered-cocoons,...
(Retaining thick-stenches and odors!),
THICK-stenches and odors, (OF their own!),
AND OF those, "previously-cocooned", IN same!,
(THOSE COCOONS DON'T GET WASHED OUT!!!),
YOU GET ZIPPED-UP,
LAYIN' ON TOP OF,
ANOTHER DEAD-MOTHERFUCKER'S,
FLUIDS AND JUICES -
Simple and plain!,
ENCASED WITHIN,
(OF AND, WITH!),
The THICK stench,
OF hard liquor and bowels!!,

And...

(That sick-fucking-imposter-doctor - the-MOST-trife - JUST MIGHT)...

Go IN there!,
IN THAT freezer!!,
THAT TRIFLIN' MOTHERFUCKER!!!,...

AND...

(((Lay HIMSELF on down!!!)))

Lay himself on down,...
ON THAT slippery cold floor!,
Amongst THOSE filthy -
"roll-'em-in-roll-'em-out" -
MOISTENED - condensation - dirty-gurney-tracks!,

AND...

(((TAKE HIMSELF A NAP!!!!!!)))

In THAT freezer!!,
AMONGST HIS FRIENDS,
a.k.a. The Dead.

'Cause...

(HE'S a crowd-pleaser!)

But...

He DON'T!

'CAUSE...

There's WORK to be done!

(((DIRTY WORK!!!)))

SICK-fucking-imposter-doctor-trifling-kind-of-WORK!!!

(COME!!! Let's have a look)...

AS...

The most trife,
Directs one of y'all five to write,
Some false-shit,
On a toe tag!,

AS...

One of the five,
(UNdirected!),
Takes the initative,
As he UNZIPS -
Bless' - "postmortem-cocoon" -
OF HER -
White disaster bag!,

As...

DANK DARK DEAD BLOOD STILL BLEEDS,
One of y'all busies himself,
As he to reads,
What's written on the containers,
Positioned up on a shelf,
Containing the final meals,
OF sick stomach contents collected,
OF internal organs removed AND inspected!!,

As...

One gets hit with the HOT taste,

IN THE BACK OF HIS THROAT,
OF his own "stomach-content-waste"!,

And...

(Psst!)...(Hey, Reader!!)...(I'LL BET in a few seconds FROM NOW!!!)...

YOU WILL BE BEGINNING,
TO FEEL a lil' bit SICK,
TO YOUR STOMACH,
YOURSELF!!,

WHEN...

(YOU GET THE VISUAL,
IMAGINING THE TEXTURE,
AND HOW IT MUST FEEL,
OF YOU UPCHUCKING,
IN THE BACK OF YOUR MOUTH!!!,
AND SWALLOWING,
THOSE SLOBBERY-HOT-CHUNKS,
RIGHT BACK DOWN SOUTH!!!)...

(But, I digress)...

And so...

With that sick-triflin'-imposter-doctor's work here ALMOST complete...

Though...(Exactly WHY he did?)...(The THINGS that he did??)...

AND...(The reason being)...(WHAT he came here TO do!!)...

(((TO YOU - THE READER - have NOT YET QUITE been revealed!!!)))...

Though...(TRUST & BELIEVE!!)...

THAT those bodies,
THAT - THAT sick-imposter-doctor-the-MOST-trife -
JUST WENT TO TOWN ON,
WERE sewn closed WITH -
THAT - thick red UNWAXED autopsy thread!!,

And...

THEY WERE SEWN UP NICE 'N TIGHT,
(By none other than THE ONE)...(((The MOST Trife!!!)))...

AND...

YOU CAN TRUST & BELIEVE,
He did so choose to use -
THAT BIG-HOOKED-silver-DURABLE -
Stainless-steel-sewing-needle -
To poke through and loop -
Cold wet skin - of the dead,
AS THEY WERE SEALED,
HE COMPULSIVELY DID SO, OVERDUE!!

((((((MUTHAFUCKIN'-RED-UNWAXED-AUTOPSY-THREAD-OY-VEY!!!!!!))))))

Though...(zippered twice).

FIRST...

Their chests and torsos.

THEN...

That of, their: "postmortem-cocoons".

And...

(OF that, white disaster bag?)...

Well...

From the outside,
IT'S APPARENT,
It's transparent,
And weird!!,

'Cause...

YOU CAN SEE the opaqueness,
Of the bloodied-insides,
((STREAKED AND SMEARED!!)),
WITH THAT,
COLD ASS,
Dank dead BLOOD!,...

((STREAKED & SMEARED!!))(OF THE bloodied-insides)
((AGAINST, AND UP!!))

(Though)...(on the bottom)...((YOU WILL FIND "ponding"))...

(((THOUGH FROZEN!!!)))(Though zippered)(And not open)...

YOU CAN SEE,
To the sides,
It's THE SAME, thereto!!,...

((FROZEN AGAINST, AND UP!!))(Deep)...((Dark!!))...(((AND, ROUGH!!!))),...

(As they)...((lay alone))...(((IN BLOOD!!!))),...

Of...dark maroon...

(Psst!)...(Hey, Reader)...(Go 'head)...

AND...

(((TAKE A LOOK!!!)))...

AT THAT "ponding" OF the blood!!

AND...

MAKE DAMN SURE,
THAT YOU TAKE A GOOD-LONG-HARD-LOOK,
AT THOSE LAYING IN THAT BLOOD "PONDING" TOO!!

(Laying there!)(((DEAD!!!)))(All alone!)(And)...(marooned).

For(You SEE!!)...

THEN IT'S back INTO the freezer!!,
OR IN a silver-stainless-steel-
heavy-handled-drawer THEY go!!,

(Psst!)...(Hey, Reader!)...

(Can YOU handle THESE TRAVELS along life's road???)...

Well, then...(Go 'head!!)...(((TAKE A LOOK!!!)))...

For...

If YOU choose to travel the wrong path?

(Psst!)...((HEY, READER!!))...(((YOU CAN BEST-BELIEVE!!!)))...

(The wrong path)...((JUST MAY HAVE YOU layin' there))...(((LIKE THAT!!!)))

AS...

They CONTINUE to - LAY-THERE-layin'-there - LIKE that!!,
(((Layin' IN that white disaster bag!!!))),
HAVING someone rotten,

((((Like one of the four YOU BROKE IN WITH to the morgue!!!!)))),
Runnin' through YOUR POCKETS!!!,
AND WRESTLING off'a YOUR - dead blue fingers - blue diamonds!!!!!,

AAAAAAND...

(Psst!)...(HEY, READER!)...

THAT'S WHAT would be called the "false profit".

AAAAAAND...

(((YOU'RE DEAD!!!)))

SOOOOOO...

YOU CAN'T stop it!!!!

AAAAAAND(AS SUCH!)...

ALL YOU CAN DO,
(((IN THAT COOLER OF A ROOM!!!))),
IS LIE THERE,
WHILE THEY'RE,
Ripping OFF YOUR heirlooms,
AND stealin' YOUR necklaces AND lockets!!!!,

'Cause...

Dependant upon,
The dead's sex,
Man or woman,
YOU JUST MAY HAVE some nut,
Employed in the morgue,
Thinkin' to themself,...

("Hmm)...(you know what???")...

("FOR being cold and dead)...((((((SHE IS a HOT GIRL!!!!!!")))))))

(Psst!)...(Hey, Reader!)...

(YOU still wanna travel the wrong path in this world??)

For...

(ONE of the four THAT YOU broke in with to the morgue)...

Well...

THAT ONE - STAYS IN LOVE,
With his love affair,
OF RIPPING-OFF - WHILE rippin'-through,
The pockets of,
THE GIRL with the peeled-off face!!!!,
(The girl...with the mermaid hair:(FOR(YOU SEE!!!)...

(THAT ONE - is an art lover!)...(In love WITH the art)...(((The art: OF the gank!)))

The art: OF no shame! (OR DISGRACE!!!!),
The art: OF STEALING your ideas!!,
(ALL while, AND ALL THE BETTER)...
THE FINE ART: OF financing THAT SHIT,...
Through SOMEONE ELSE'S bank!!!,

AS...

(The runnin' of tha' pockets - for THAT ONE - NEVER stops!!)

(Psst!)...(Hey, Reader!)...

YEAH, YOU'RE gettin' it now!!,

(As I knew YOU WOULD somehow;)
THIS POEM ain't pretty!,

BUT...

(((It's pretty AT the top!!!)))

And...(Just so that YOU know)...

(((THE ONLY WAY I WRITE IS UNAPOLOGETICALLY!!!)))

AND...(Psst!)...(Hey, Reader!)...(I have a question OF YOU to ask!)...

(Read what's directly below)...AAAAAAAND...(((Then YOU do the math!!!)))...

(((I'VE DESCRIBED MY WRITINGS AS "UNAPOLOGETICALLY" - LOOOOOOONG BEFORE the word "Unapologtically" BECAME TRENDY!!!)))

AAAAAAND...

(Writing THAT WAY)...(Psst!)...(Hey, Reader)...(Guess what??)...

(((((((I WILL NEVER STOP!!!!!!!)))))))...((((((((WELCOME to MY world!!!!!!!)))))))

AND SO...

(From ME, to YOU)...

"WHEN YOU bought MY book?,
YEAH,...I KNEW,...what I was gettin' YOU into!",...

AAAAAAND...

"It NOW looks like,
YOU NOW know it too!!",...

A: Straight-Up - TO BE Sure -
YOU-Didn't-See-This-Shit-Comin' -
BUT-THIS-IS-HOW-Bad-I-Want-It -
Trip To The Morgue!!!"

(But, I digress)...

For(YOU see!)...

(After some time)...(though)...(not SO MUCH time)...

That sick-trife-imposter-doctor,
Did indeed,
Do his shit,
AND handled his biz!,
((((Before YOU and the odd four!!!!)))),...
Go creepin' back out THAT unassuming door,
The one with an unassuming plastic sign,
With recessed lettering in white,
Labled: "MORGUE".

THOUGH...(bagged-up)...(back in the morgue)...

Was an extra-thick,
Extra-husky,
Extra-red,
Plastic trash bag,...

Left tied up.
((RETIED up!!)).
Previously,...tied up.
(((PREVIOUSLY, left labeled-up: "INCINERATOR"!!!))),...

And...

(Before ALL Y'ALL broke out on some "SEE YA' LATER"!!!!!)...

Replaced at the bottom,
((ALL KINDS OF FUNKY 'N TART!!)),
Of a wheeled-industrial-strength-canvas laundry cart,
WAS THAT extra-thick-red-trash bag!,
As it was placed at the bottom of that,
Under other thick-red-bags,
ALL OF WHICH containing,
Body parts in variations,...

SUCH AS...

(Stones from kidney to gall!!)...

AS...

THAT CART was left parked,
In that bottom-level hospital hall,
Just outside the door,
With that - recessed-white-lettered-black-plastic-sign -
Labeled: "MORGUE"!,

WITH...

EVERY ITEM,
White lab coat and uniform,
In its proper-local,
It was back,
((JUST AS it was before!!)),

Though...

(NOT that spool of RED thread 'n shit that triflin'-imposter-doctor gripped!!)

AND...

(He's MOVIN' how HE BE movin' jack!)

Soooooo...

(YOU BEST TRY AND KEEP UP!!!)...

'CAUSE...

(((HE'S BURNIN' that Nigerian incense!!!)))

And(AS FOR)...

THAT TRIFLIN' SHIT,
That triflin'-imposter-doctor did,
Back there,
In the morgue??,...

Well...

Bless, was zippered thrice.

First...

There was the removal of her internal organs!

But...

(YOU have to understand!)...

It wasn't til' AFTER,
That triflin'-doctor-imposter,
With a scalpel in a steady hand,
Gave Bless a "Y" incision!!,

(He made a clean run)...(Her blood ran)...

And...

(DON'T get it twisted!)...

The imposter-doctor's triflin' scalpel point positionin' -
((In the vicinity of her collarbone's "AC joint")) -

Was JUST the beginnin'!!,...

As...

He made,
Layered flesh,
Fat,
And red meat,
Gape.

As...

The splits in her pecs,
OF her chest-flesh met,
One. At. A. Time,...
JUST BELOW her breastplate!!,

After(and THEN!)...

That imposter-doc-MOST-triflin',
Twisted that scalpel blade,
AS HE MADE IT - MAKE ITS WAY,
All the way down 'n 'round her navel,
He, DID SO, MAKE IT SNAKE!!!,

After(AND THEN!!)...

Gaped-layered flesh,
Fat,
And red meat,
Hung down over the sides,
Two at a time,
To at a time,
Knowing together,
He'll have to heft them shitz back up together,
Knowing he'll have to pull them shitz together,

OF her flesh,
KNOWING he'll be sewing together!!,

As...

THAT imposter-doctor-MOST-trife,
Had already made his decision,
That he'd be givin' Bless' "Y" incision -
"A - THICK-RED-
MAXIMUM-TRACTION-UNWAXED-
AUTOPSY-THREADED-
STAINLESS-STEEL-STURDY-
HOOKED-NEEDLED-BACK-TOGETHER - SPLICE",...
(COMPLIMENTS, OF THAT IMPOSTER-DOCTOR..."THE MOST TRIFE"!!!)...

But...

(YOU HAVE TO understand!)...

THE process OF the plan!

(OF Bless' autopsy)...(((YOU attended!!!)))

FOR(YOU SEE!!!)...

Didn't none of that happen,
Til' after,
That imposter-doctor,
Implemented,
The use of a white-'n-wide -
red-numbered-'n-lined -
"barrelled-of-circumference" -
long-'n-thick -
needled-syringe,

For...

(The drainage of urine!)...

Into Bless' bladder,
That triflin'-doctor-imposter,
Punctured dead skin,

As...

He stuck it deep down within!

And(then)...

With that,
THICK 'N RED -
UNWAXED -
AUTOPSY THREAD,
That imposter-doctor-most-triflin',
USED IT to tie off the ends,
(once removed!),
OF Bless' large intestines,
To ensure the CONTAINMENT,
OF ALL OF HER excrement!!,

THEN...

(While back in that cooler of a room,
What that imposter-doctor chose,
WHILE STILL BEING WATCHED,
BY THE SPIRITS THAT ROSE!,
While he was STILL breathing in,
STILL TO BE -
forever-without-question-
mucus-membrane-embedded -
ALL UP AND IN -

the linings of his sinuses,
WHERE THE STENCH OF CHEMICALS 'N BOWELS,
HUNG AS IT FROZE!!!),...

Well...

Of her fingers and toes,
Down to and through and off the bone,
He snipped!

Then...
He moved onto her palms,
And the soles of her feet!!,

As...

He: "scalpelled-them-off",
dead skin split,
peeled,
and lifted-off,
clean!,

And...

(There will be NO indentifying Bless,
Through her dental records)...

'CAUSE...

That rottin'-imposter-doctor,
    Removed ALL OF HER teeth!,

And...

(((ALL OF THAT,
WAS PLACED INTO THAT,
RED "INCINERATOR" BAG!!!))),

BUT...

NOT UNTIL,
AFTER THE REMOVAL,
OF EVERYTHING,
SKELETAL AND REMOVABLE!,
(Of, SOME - Layin'-There-Cold-Wet-
Blue-Naked-And-Dead -
MOTHERFUCKER -
LAYIN' THERE -
DEAD-NAKED -
FULL FRONTAL!,
(OH, YOU'RE IN IT NOW!)...
(AIN'T NO TURNING BACK NOW!)...
(AIN'T NO TIME TO BE A COWARD!!!)...

'CAUSE...

By that triflin'-imposter-doctor,
EVERYTHING REMOVABLE AND SKELETAL,
WAS OSCILLATED-AUTOPSIED-SAWED-UP -
SLICED 'N DICED,
DOWN TO A -
Fine-skulldust-sawdust-dust-mite-particle-powder!!!,

And so...

With that imposter-doctor,
NOT being new to this,
It didn't take him,
NO MORE than an hour!,

Which led...

To as much DNA,
Out of Bless' jugulars,
By THAT imposter-doctor,
EACH ONE,
BEING BLED!!,

WHICH LED...

To Bless' blood,
Deep-dark-and-dank,
Flowin' down til' it reached,
That autopsy table's drain,
Positioned down,...
By Bless' TOELESS FEET!!,

WHICH LED...

AS THAT -
DANK-DARK-DEAD-BLOOD - STANK,
FLOWED, AND STREAKED -
DOWN TO AND THRU,
THAT AUTOPSY TABLE'S -
WHY'D-THEY-HAVE-TO-
MAKE-THIS-SO-THICK-'N-ODDLY-TRANSPARENT -
DRAINAGE TUBE!,

OF WHICH...

WHEN SEEN THROUGH,
BY WHICH,
ALL IN THE ROOM!!!!,
(OF WHICH),...
(INCLUDED YOU!!!!!),
ALL BUT,
That triflin'-imposter-doctor,

(And possibly NOW YOU!),
IT ALL BUT,
KICK-STARTED GAGGIN'-ACTIONS -
AND HURLIN' -
FOR CERTAIN!!!,

BUT...

(IT ONLY GOT WORSE!!!)...

WHEN...

Bless' DANK BLOOD -
CAUSED THAT AUTOPSY ROOM'S -
CENTRALLY LOCATED -
ROUND-ESTUARY-FLOOR-GRATE -
FOR DRAINAGE,
TO FLOOD!,

BUT...

(IT GOT WORSE!!)...

WHEN...

THE CENTRALLY-LOCATED-
ROUND-ESTUARY-FLOOR-GRATE-FOR-DRAINAGE -
STARTED WITH ITS SPITTIN' 'N SPURTIN' -
OF: "SHEETS OF DANKNESS" -
(AND LEST WE FORGET!) -
THE "BLOOD CURTAINS"!!,

AND(FOR CERTAIN),...

(IT GOT MUCH WORSE!!!),...
WHEN...
THAT ESTUARY-OF-A-FLOOR-GRATE MADE,

ALL BUT,
THAT TRIFLIN'-IMPOSTER-DOCTOR,
CAPITULATE!!!,

'CAUSE...

THEIR FUTILE ATTEMPTS,
TO NOT START HURLIN',
WERE NO LONGER WORKIN'!!!,

(FROM JUST THE SOUNDS ALONE BEING MADE!!!)...

CAUSE...

THAT DAMN DRAINAGE GATE,
WOULDN'T STOP,...
REGURGITATIN' 'N GURGLIN'!!!,...

After(And then)...

There was the placement of in,
That RED "INCINERATOR" BAG,
OF everythin'...but tha' skin,...
OF THAT - COLD-WET-
BLUE-NAKED-HOLLOWED-OUT-MESS -
(OF A MOTHERFUCKER!),
THAT Bless,
WAS 'BOUT TO GET,
ZIPPERED-UP IN!!!,

Though...

NOT BEFORE SO,
With that UNWAXED -
THICK 'N RED -
AUTOPSY THREAD,

That triflin'-imposter-doctor,
ZIPPERED-UP Bless',
CHEST AND TORSO -
WITH MAXIMUM TRACTION,
OF HIS SEWING ACTION -
NICE 'N TIGHT -
HE DID SO!!!,

And(then)...

THAT imposter-doctor-MOST-TRIFE,
"Cocooned her" inside,
Sealed all-up-in,
THAT - HOLLOWED-OUT-MOTHERFUCKER'S -
COLD-WET-BLUE-SKIN!!,

AND...

(HE DID SO, NICE 'N TIGHT!!)...

WHICH LED...

(TO Bless, BEING ZIPPERED twice!!)...

And so...(THEN),...

(THAT imposter-doctor-MOST-TRIFE,...ZIPPERED HER THRICE!!!)...

For,...

Once BACK IN her white disaster bag,
She got zipped back up,...

BUT...(THIS TIME!),...

BLESS,...

EVEN HAD,...
HER VERY OWN,...
TOE TAG!,

(WRITTEN WITH SOME FALSE SHIT ON IT!)

And...

It was hangin' off just the lil' bit,
Of what was left of her right big toe -
gingerly-looped-over-and-placed - as such,
By that trife-imposter-doctor - he did so!,

After(And then)...

A heavy handled stainless steel drawer,
She was slid in,

(Bless her heart!)...(and try not to cry!)...

As...

Bless,
By that imposter-doctor-MOST-trife,
FEET FIRST,...
WAS SLID INSIDE!!

DEATH'S CONDENSATION

At a table of three,
One begins to notice,
One is not quite right,
The one seated to his right,

As one asks one,
The one to his left,
"To dine on some swine if he wants?",
('Cause somes a lil' left!),

As for one,
It has begun,
A grayish-white color,
The facial hue is turning to,

The one manages to his feet,
One golden hour to manage,
To the other one,
It appears to be,

Upon two feet the one teeters,
Upon rising from his seat,
Upon the floor the one has fallen,
Upon a slow lean,

One rushes to that one,
Springing up from his chair,
Checking that one for the pulse,
That isn't there!,

The one now can only glare,
Into the non-communicative eyes,

Of the one now lying there,

Of the one on the floor,
As for that one's eyes,
They remain fixed on the baseboard,

As the one remained on his side,
One remained glaring,
Into the dementia of his eyes,

To the one it's permissable,
To think that when death enters you,
It makes itself visible,
When your entire body it travels through,

Absorbing into every humanly cell,
And when death enters your head,
Death steals the color from your face,
And then throws that away as well,

Then just to make sure all know,
Of you coming back,
There is no hope,

Of your being,
Being gone for good,
Controlling the conversation,...

Color from your dead face,
Death collects,
In the form of condensation,

For death,
Don't EVER need,
YOUR permission!,

FOR death,
DON'T wait,
For YOU to say "When"!,

With YOUR dead eyes,
Death opens them,

Sprinkling acrost a grayish-white,
Death coats them,

Two things for one,
One has just learned,

One has just died,
Right before his eyes,

And the other one,
Just doesn't seem overly concerned,

The one says,
"This one's dead.",

Placing his one hand,
On the dead one's forehead,

The other one,
Beginning to laugh it up,
Tells the one, "He's fine.",

As life's beginning to,
Filter up through,
The condensation of the dead one's eyes,

And so...

At the table of three,
All three are just fine,

Each one of the three,
Dining on some swine,

As the one laughs and says,
"I told you he ain't dead!,
He does this all the time!"

AND THERE SHE LAY

(One crazy)...AND...(One filled with anger)...

The crazy one,
Hops down outta his two axle tanker,

(Up on the ninth floor)...(Of a parking garage)...(He did so park)...

As...

The one with anger,
Pulls in nice 'n smooth next to the tanker,

And(Then)...

Grandly exits outta his,
'53 Buick Skylark!,

For(You See)...

(They've come to pay their respects)...(to the Heathen)...(at the top of the steps)...

And...

(Before they enter the stairwell)...(BOTH take a deep breath)...

As...

(They both walk towards)...(a battleship-gray door)...

And there she lay,
Where the steps just seem to go away,
Up from that ninth floor stairwell landing,
Fifteen steps to the top,
Like some cruel joke or mercy,
Those stairwell steps just abruptly stop!,

And there she lay,
Up there where the steps turn,
Into a steel platform urn,
Just below a cement ceiling,
(Can't sit - barely enough room for head clearance!),
And there she lay,
Amongst everything painted battleship-gray!,

And there she lay,
Amongst the multicolored baggies,
Amongst the bent spoons, the needles,
Up there amongst where the ashy,
Ripped soda cans in half,
(Ripped 'em right in half LIKE it was nuthin'),...
(((ALL for the purpose of COOKIN' UP sumfin'!!!))),...

And there she lay,
Amongst the tiny particles of narcotic,
Of whom - some addict's misfortune,
Fingertips burning from the Bic,
Down on their hands and knees,
Lookin' for that lil' sumfin'-sumfin' tiny 'n tasty,
Such as a lil' tiny piece of rock,
After some addict got all "Highed-up",
And unfathomably let a tiny piece of rock drop!,
(AND NEVER did spot it!),
(WHICH STILL REQUIRED) -
Painfully-immeasurably-painstaking-effort!,
To find a lil' sumfin'-sumfin' impossible to measure!,

Though...(Have NO fear!)...

THAT tiny "tasty treat" DIDN'T get away!!

For(YOU SEE)...

(((It's down there IN THAT pungent urine stain!!!)))

And there she lay,
Amongst the shit and blood,
And there she lay,
In silent observance and love,

Up those steps,
Go the crazy,
And the angry,
And there she lay,
Respects to pay,

(And there she lay)...(In a lovely purple dress)...(Hiked up over her head)...

((('CAUSE MOTHERFUCKERS ARE FUCKED-UP LIKE THAT!!!)))

And there she lay,
Flat on her back,
And there she lay,
Amongst soda cans ripped in half,

And there she lay,
Up on that battleship-gray platform,...

(One crazy)...(One angry)...(THOUGH)...(BOTH on the same page!)...

ON HOW they both chose to pay,
Their respects and morn!!,...

And there she lay,
Her porcelain white skin,

Separated in half,
In half - ((JUST THINK ABOUT THAT!!)) -

In half - ((HER SKIN)) - was divided in!!

And there she lay,
Lookin' like she's laying on top,
Of the dark dead blood of a corpse,
Her lividity,...
(((DARK 'N DIRTY LIKE motor oil!))),
And there she lay,
LOOKING JUST LIKE,...
SHE'S laying on top of the fucked-up potting soil OF HER life!,

And(then)...(YOU SEE)...

The angry one grits his teeth!,
AS HE pulls her dress down nice 'n neat,
UPON seeing the fentanyl patches,
STILL CLUTCHED IN the rigors of her teeth!!!,

AS...

The crazy one douses her body,
With gas from that tanker truck hose!,

And(THEN)...

The one that's angry,
Leaves that hose over the railing hanging,
Down the stairwell gasoline flows,...
Letting the gas make its way,
Down ten flights leading up to hell,
Painted battleship-gray!,

AND SO...

(The crazy one)...(hands the angry one)...(the last one)...(out from one)...

Box of wooden matches.

And(As Such)...

(The angry one)...(Struck that bitch)...(As so)...

And(AS SUCH)...

(((OFF THE TOP OF THAT PARKING GARAGE THE TOP DID BLOW!!!)))
'CAUSE...

(((FROM SOMETHING)))...((EVERYBODY'S GOTTA DIE))...
(sometime)...

For(You See)...

It was those two handrail guides,
Coiled and snaked,
Painted battleship-gray,
That led them,
The first time,
The three of them,
RIGHT ON UP,...to the end of the line.

STILL BORN

Death, I think,...

It's just black oblivion.
But you don't even know you're there.

You don't know that you were ever alive.
And you don't know that you're dead.

You're just dead.
And it doesn't even matter,
That you were ever alive.

It's black. It's an oblivion. It's everywhere.

Death, I think,...

It's like a baby that dies,
Before it gets born.

They don't know that they were alive.
And they don't know that they have died.

They're just dead.

Dead and all alone in the dark.
Just like the day when they died all alone.

Dead baby. Alone. In the darkness of the womb.

Death, I think,...

Is like dead babies.
Just like dead babies in that black oblivion of the womb.

They don't even know that they are dead.
And they don't even know that they are all alone.

Death, I think,...

Will be like that.
I can't wait to get there.

And...

(Let ME - tell YOU - somethin' about the dead!)...

Millenniums from THIS millennium,
And millenniums beyond THOSE millenniums still ahead,...

And...

Millenniums BEYOND those millenniums,
BEYOND THOSE millenniums,...

THE. DEAD. WILL. STILL. BE. DEAD.

OUGHT

MR. OFFICER

Mr. Officer, I can't breathe!,
WITH my neck FULL of knee!,
Before I die,
Can you show me,
Some compassion, please?

Mr. Officer, I'M PISSIN' MYSELF!!!,
DON'T YOU KNOW,
MY NECK FULL OF KNEE,
IS BAD FOR MY HEALTH???,
CAN'T YOU SEE THAT,
FROM WAY UP ON,
YOUR HIGH HORSE SHELF??,
Mr. Officer, can't you see MY LIFE,
ALSO has,...value and wealth?,

Mr. Officer, WITH my neck FULL of knee,
NOW MY STOMACH HURTS!!!,
YOU GOT ME CALLIN' OUT FOR MY MA'MA!!!,
'Cause, I KNOW, I'M 'BOUT TO leave this earth!,
Mr. Officer, WHAT YOU'RE DOIN',
AND, WHAT I'M ACCUSSED OF,
TELL ME!!! ...Which one is worse?,

Mr. Officer, don't you see,
ALL THOSE cell phones???,
WITH my neck FULL of knee,
NOW I GOT BLOOD COMIN' OUT MY NOSE!!!,
Mr. Officer, I just want to see,...

Someone come help me,...
BEFORE my eyes close,

Mr. Officer, you're killing me!,
In broad daylight!,
On a city street!,
Mr. Officer, you're killing me!,
In broad daylight!,
On a city street!,
WITH a smirk on your face!,
And with my neck FULL of knee!,

Mr. Officer, do you know what YOU just did?,
YOU JUST gave birth,
To a NEW GENERATION,
OF revolutionary kids!,
Mr. Officer, WITH my neck FULL of knee,
THAT'S WHAT YOU DID!!!,
YOU just gave birth,
To a NEW generation,
Of REVOLUTIONARY kids!,

Mr. Officer,...I CAN'T BREATHE!!!,
WITH MY NECK FULL OF KNEE!!!!!!,
Before I die,...
Can YOU,...
Show ME,...
SOME compassion,...please?

TAKE THE KNEE

I ain't askin' for shit,
And sure as fuck don't need your respect,
Ain't no please massa' please,
I'm takin' your knee off my neck,

Kap took a knee,
Just askin' for respect,
I ain't askin' for shit!,
I'm takin' the knee off my neck!,

All four,
In full uniform,
Cut my brother's air off,
Like it has happened,
So many times before,

On THAT DAY...

THAT SHIT officially got old!,
'Cause THOSE FOUR were TOO bold!!!!,
Like THEY got it like that!!!!,
Like THEY KNEW the system got their back!!!!,

Like THEY KNEW EVERYONE filming,
On their phones would just hang back!,
Like THEY KNEW EVERYONE would be,
TOO afraid TO attack!,

And it WOULD'NT HAVE BEEN about,
Breakin' the law!,
It WOULD HAVE BEEN about,
The law BREAKIN' the law!!!!,

It WOULD HAVE BEEN about,
PUTTING A STOP to just about,
The SADDEST thing,
That WE as human beings,
HAVE EVER SAW!!!,

And there BEST NOT BE no NEXT time!,
'Cause I WILL do - What I HAVE TO do,
EVEN IF THAT MEANS,
Being gunned down,
IN FRONT OF ALL OF Y'ALL!!!,

'CAUSE...

There's a NEW playing field,
And THAT'S the field I'm playing on!,
BUT I AIN'T PLAYIN'!,
And THIS will be MY new norm!,
I AIN'T askin' for shit!,
I AIN'T askin' for reform!,

'CAUSE...

THAT SHIT AIN'T NEVER,
EVER, EVER, EVER, GONNA,
HAPPEN NO MORE!!!,

I'm on deck,
Try me NEXT!,
WATCH ME put these,
Human rights abusers IN-CHECK,
WHEN I take YOUR knee off MY neck!,

There's a NEW playing field,
BUT I AIN'T PLAYIN'!,

NOW raise YOUR fist in the air,
If you know what I'M sayin'!,

THIS is what the system has,
Systemically created,
Taking a knee was never about,
The flag being denegrated,

Taking a knee was never disrespect for,
Soldiers at home or on a foriegn shore,
Diversionary tactics turned it into all that,
Yet ANOTHER knee on the neck of the black!,

I ain't askin' FOR shit!,
And SURE AS FUCK don't need your respect!,
AIN'T NO please massa' please,
I'M taking YOUR knee off MY neck!,

Kap took a knee,
Just askin' for respect,
I AIN'T ASKIN' FOR SHIT!,
I'M takin' the knee off MY neck!,

All four,
In full uniform,
Cut my brother's air off,
Like it has happened,
So many times before!,

And don't you EVER let ME see THAT shit!,
I'll kick YOUR head off YOUR shoulders WHEN I run in!,
THAT AIN'T BULLSHIT - NOT EVEN A LIL' BIT!!!!,

FUCK REFORM!!!!,
THOSE FOUR created a NEW playing field!!!!,

And THAT'S the field I'M playing on!,

Now read the next line slowly,...
BUT. I. AIN'T. PLAYIN'.
AIN'T NO please massa' please,
NOW raise YOUR fist in the air,
IF you know what I'm sayin'!

TAUT

RATZ IN THE WALLZ

I swear for God,
I ain't havin' it no more,
You want it - You got it!,
A gangsta's answering my door!,

AND I swear for God!,
The bloods gonna pour!!!,
'Cause I got ratz in the wallz,
And cowardz in the floor,

Ain't nothin' new,...
I'm back to using again,
And I'm being watched,
'Cause they THINK I'm trafficking,

THEM PEOPLE are funny!,
They know I AIN'T got money!,
BUT they pray to God I'M the connect!,
So MY LIFE they inspect!!!,

Again, and again, AND AGAIN,
They DON'T stop!,
They WON'T feel safe,
TIL' my jail cell's locked!,

WHY else would they,
Keep comin' for me???,
Ha! It's YOUR tax dollars,
AND IT'S a spending spree!,

I bet the taxpayers,
SURE WOULD BE pissed off!,
Infrared lights in the dark,
Come with a sneeze and a cough,

Yeah,
THAT dirty little whore,
GOT ME paranoid,
OF vice snappin' pics,
LIKE I'M Pretty Boy Floyd!,

OF bugs in my shoes,
AND IN my clothes LIKE ticks!,
OF MY cell being tapped,
'CAUSE I HEAR WHEN IT CLICKS!!!,

Of the neighbors next door,
And apartment below,
With their ears pressed to the ceiling,
While standing on the stove,

Of Feds in my attic,
Or a secret society,
'Cause I CAN hear them through the wallz,
AS they try to spy on me,

AND THERE AIN'T NOTHING WORSE,
THEN a friendly look,
From your so-called boy,
WHEN the judge threw the book!,

BUT THEY BITCH-MADE!!!,
So THEY turn state,
WEARING wires and shit,
SO AS to seal your fate!,

BUT you ON that whore,
Peeping shit ALL night,
So you second-guess,
But,...traffic AIN'T moving right!,

I swear for God!,
I AIN'T having it no more,
YOU WANT IT - YOU GOT IT,
A gangsta's answering MY door!,

AND I swear for God,
THE BLOOD'S GONNA POUR,
'Cause I got RATZ in the wallz,
And COWARDZ in tha floor,

AND my front tooth is chipped,
From THAT dirty little bitch,
From clinching my jaw til it's sore,
And from eating that DIRTY LITTLE WHORE,

TEN DAYS I was spun,
Swear for God,...WISH I HAD A GUN!!!,
Hearing whispers IN the wallz at night,
WITH my jaw clinched tight!,

That whore AIN'T NO joke!,
Especially when you smoke,
Or doin' hot rails,
CARS CREEP PAST THE CRIB LIKE SNAILS,

And I'LL BE DAMNED,
My "friends" ARE working for the "man"!,
As they creep and they crawl,
Swear for God,...they're behind tha wallz,

Secret entrances and videos,
Watchin' me are my foes,
Silhouettes outside my windows,
DAMN anything goes,

AND MY GUT FEELING,
THESE nigga's GOT peep holes in the ceiling,
And I swear there's a secret door,
Up under my floor,

And EVERY TIME I go outside,
They SNEAK IN my crib and hide,
And my watches and shit,
NEVER used to look like this!,

DUPLICATE AND SWITCH is their plan,
PUT THERE by the "man",
Damn push came to shove,
'Cause I got WHITE PAINT on my rug!!!,
And I KNOW that shit's NEW,
PEEPIN' SHIT IS WHAT I DO,

Incriminating texts and voicemails,
Y'all THINK I'm a dumb black male,
I'M HIP TO YOUR REINDEER GAMES,
Y'ALL AIN'T EVEN TALKING THE SAME,...
Did you cop and how much?,
Did you get it from such n' such?,
And what time will you be home?,
And ALL THIS over the phone!,
Don't matter if I'm right or just spun,...
'CAUSE I AIN'T SELL SHIT TO NO ONE,

I SWEAR FOR GOD,

I AIN'T HAVING IT NO MORE,
Y'ALL WANT IT - Y'ALL GOT IT!!!!!!,
A GANGSTA'S ANSWERING MY DOOR!!!!!!,
AND I SWEAR FOR GOD,
THE BLOOD'S GONNA POUR!!!!!!,
'CAUSE I GOT RATZ IN THE WALLZ,
AND COWARDZ IN THA' FLOOR!!!!!!

FACEBOOK TOUGH GUY

I'm just a Facebook Tough Guy,
I really ain't about nothin',
All those red carpet pics are photoshopped,
I'm just out here steady frontin',

I already think I'm at the top,
No I don't think I have to pay my dues,
And if you believe that shit?,
Please believe these ain't my tail cut gator shoes!,

And no that ain't my "Six-Fiddy",
'Cause you never see me drivin' in it,
Just like his diamond pinky rings,
We all know all his shit is rented!,

I know my girl ain't bad,
(And I say that with a sarcastic frown:(
It ain't like we can show up ANYWHERE,
(AND shut that motherfucker down;)

It really ain't my style,
To acknowledge you haters,
Y'all stay on some - "Look what I got!"
While I stay on some - "See ya' later!",

For(YOU see)...

It's really all just a big waste of time!,
But if YOU? - Got it in YOU??,
Come see about me!,
'Cause I ain't hard to find!,

(Psst)...(HEY, HATERS!!!)...

Just break your fucking neck,
Looking up at,
The other level,
I'LL BE up here on my grind!!!

MONSTER

Dogs and cats all run and flee,
And they all flee from me,
What you get is what you see,
'Cause I'm the monster in your dreams,

Misunderstood by the world,
I'm cool with that,
But I can see the beauty in a dead bat,
Kept him as my pet 'cause we wear all black,
I sleep on top of graves flat on my back,

Birds they all fly away,
So that they may live another day,
High up in a tree they keep an eye on me,
'Cause I'm the monster in THEIR dreams,

WHEN you're different the world AIN'T your home,
King Kong just wanted to be left alone,
Frankenstein was chased by angry droves,
I'm just a monster in wolf clothes,

Nothing is ever as it seems,
The world made the Hulk bust its seams,
(((DAMN THIS WORLD CAN BE SO MEAN!!!))),
'Cause WE'RE the MONSTERS in YOUR dreams,

Sheeps of the world believe EVERYTHING that's said,
Robots believe everything they're FED,
ME and the Boogeyman live under EVERY bed,
I'M JUST A MONSTER THAT THE WORLD BRED,

Monsters, we have an ugly world in our sight,

Monsters, YOUR world is OUR plight,
Monsters, WE DON'T SLEEP, WE count the seconds at night,
And YOU sheep, COUNT ME at night,

I LIVE IN THE DARK, my sarcophagus,
And I LIVE AND BREATHE the Apocalypse,
Ever sleep on a grave and feel an ice cold mist?,
YOU PUSSIES don't know what you're missing,
(THAT SHIT WAS BLISS!!!),

YOU snakes in the grass, you're ALL beneath my feet,
And YOUR kids YOU TELL, it's babies I EAT,
Day of Blood, I'll carve you up when I pull my knife out its sheath,
AND I'LL TELL YOU THAT SHIT THROUGH GRITTED TEETH,

The world MADE monters by not showing enough love,
The world made monsters BY NOT giving enough hugs,
You cowards NEED monsters to feel better,
Like a fiend needs drugs,
AND ON MY SOUL, YOU MOTHERFUCKERS,
There can NEVER be enough blood,

When you're different the world AIN'T your home,
King Kong just wanted to be LEFT ALONE,
Frankenstein was CHASED BY ANGRY DROVES,
I'M just a monster IN wolf clothes,

NOTHING is EVER as it seems,
The WORLD MADE the Hulk bust its seams,
DAMN this world can be SO mean,
'Cause WE'RE the monsters IN YOUR DREAMS.

McRIB

Dehydrated, pupils dilated,
By the law infiltrated,
Through those high,
On my trust-level that I rated,

My dirty little whore,
Had me stimulated,
Paid informants working overtime,
To alter my destiny to be ill-fated,

"Solo Dolo", I stay,
'Cause these females play games,
Witcha' DUSTY asses,
Like your shit is clean slated!,

And I know,
After I've made it,
It will feel so good,
To be the world's MOST hated!,

Please believe I don't sweat,
From a bitch's hot breath,
Fell on deaf ears and jaded,
Hoes got suffocated,

Sadly, though,
Through muddy waters I've waded,
Lifeline on a white line,
Stayed afloat - self-medicated,

Pistol grip Mossberg,
Yeah I sprayed it,

Caught the dragon's tail,
Damn right I slaid it!,

Cut my dreads off,
So now I fade it,
Gonna grow 'em back,
New town/New look - that's how I played it,

740il straight cash,
That's how I paid it,
I'd roll through any hood,
And communities that were gated,

Puff - Puff - Pass,
Keep the cadance,
Chicken shitz,
S.W.A.T Team NEVER raided!,

Trust for heart bust,
That's how they traded,
Heart strings,
Tattered and fray-did,

But somehow - for a female,
I still have respect - wanna take a guess?,
'Cause God took my rib,
AND THAT'S HOW y'all were created!

FALSE PROFIT

False profit,
You can't stop it,
Man I'm burning rubber,
Straight out the cockpit,

I'm out to get,
All that I can get,
Makin' money the fast way,
That's a sure bet,

Let's go make some moves,
Ain't got shit to prove,
I'll make you make the news,
The profit is fake,
Got money to make,
I need new tennis shoes,

I need new everything,
I want everything,
And YOU lookin' like a "cop caller",
That's why I'M quick to swing!,

I'll break your jaw so you can't sing,
Just give up your watch,
And your wallet,
AND I'M TAKING that ring!,

And I ain't chicken shit,
And I ain't no piece of shit,
'Cause I ain't on some coward shit,
I won't pretend to be your friend,
To get in close to get your ends,

(That AIN'T the work of men!),
(YOU LIFELONG low-life deadbeat dad motherfuckers!!!),
That AIN'T the work of men!,

I'll just straight-up give you that look,
The look you give me,
I know you shook!,
(Quick-fast JUST like that!),
YOUR heart is took!,

The false profit,
You can't stop it,
Now start peeling off your paper,
LIKE a good book!,

False profit,
You can't stop it,
Man I'm burning rubber,
Straight out the cockpit!,

I'm out to get,
All that I can get,
Makin' money the fast way,
That's a sure bet!,

Got to make some moves,
Not much left to lose,
Fuck it,
My daughter needs new tennis shoes.

CASTING CALL

I used to eat out the trash can,
Knocking ashes off,
The fried eggs,
And the ribs, man!,

Don't get it twisted,
I ain't always floss,
So I made myself,
Into a motherfuckin' boss!,

Yes, indeed,
I used to get it in,
With my Nephew,
And with some so-called "friends",

But in the end,
There ain't nobody like me,
Everybody fake as fuck,
And a scam to me,

"Bros" AIN'T bros and "fam" AIN'T fam,
Wear a fake face,
To get in my pockets,
Is all they're good for, man!,

Days long gone,
Since I used to walk with Chris to the mall,
All grown up don't mean you've grown,
Most still don't stand tall,

Fifty-years old,
And now I see the truth,

My Mom used to school me,
Back in the days of Roots,

“Rod, you can’t entirely trust everyone,
Not even your best friend.,
And don’t put all your trust in them,
Or it will happen again.”,

So now I can’t trust anyone,
Your world made me this way,
EVERYTHING is black and white,
To me there AIN’T no gray!,

Hold on to what you know is real,
And you won’t get ripped off today,
And don’t be shocked if shit pops off,
Your faulty world made me this way,

“Day of Blood” love,
Is the REALIST love of all,
Bled it in a book,
So y’all don’t become my casting call.

POPULAR

I'm popular,
I said, I'm popular,
(NOT what you may think!),
But on the tip you ain't NEVER heard!,

I can't even go to the laundromat,
WITHOUT being trailed by windows tinted black,
And "THEY" so fucking whack!,
Eat my ass!,
DON'T approach!,
IF YOU KNOW WHAT'S GOOD FOR YOU,
STAY THE FUCK BACK!!!,

"THEY" MUST want to see my draws drop to the floor,
When I'm taking my draws out the dryer door!,
I peeped YOU creepin' in through the laundromat door,
Fuck 'round I'll get the drop when you get drawed down on!,

I'm popular,
I said, I'm popular,
(NOT what you may think!),
But on the tip you ain't NEVER heard!,

I pull into a gas station,
Gas pumps are vacant like an old southern plantation,
Next thing you know the whole lot is gridlocked!,
"THEY" come in LIKE a seagull flock!,

I walk in,
I walk out,
With some powerade,
And some candy bars,

AND "THESE" CLOWN ASS MOTHERFUCKERS,
ARE STILL SITTING IN THEIR CARS!!!,
AND NOT A ONE OF 'EM HAVE PUMPED NO GAS,
ALL Y'ALL MOTHERFUCKERS CAN EAT MY ASS!!!,

I'm popular,
I said, I'm popular,
(NOT what you may think!),
But on the tip you ain't NEVER heard!,

And I can't even go get my driver's license renewed,
WITHOUT being followed by "YOU KNOW WHO"!!!,
Staties on the berm,
Same tinted bitch stay followin' 'cause today's their turn,

I walk in,
I walk out,
With a brand new license,
AND THERE "THEY" ARE,
THICK LIKE LICE,
LIKE THE FUCKIN' LICE "THEY" ARE!!!,
Can't even have a smoke,
WITHOUT a fixed-wing flying DIRECTLY over my car!,

I'm popular,
I said, I'm popular,
(NOT what you may think!),
But on the tip you ain't NEVER heard!,

And before I drive my lady to work,
My lady wanted to make a stop first,
'Cause my lady wanted to buy me a birthday cake!,
Worrrd! This'll be great!,

So we pull-in, park, and walk-in,

Walk-in smooth as I do - (BUT inside I'm hidin' my grin:)
And so - my lady bought me a chocolate jawn,
With Raiders colors - the cake was written on!,
Swear for God - WE can't even go to Whole Foods!,
Parked in the cut in the lot across from us is,..."YOU KNOW WHO"!!!,

Now...

(Pay attention VERY carefully!)

AS(For)...

IF a cop just-so-happens to be of me within a close proxinity?,...

AND...

ARE doing their job - to "Protect and Serve" - with thee UTMOST of integrity?,...

Well...

(A negative word FROM ME - YOU WILL never hear a peep!)

HOWEVER...

(((SINCE I'M SICK OF THE HARASSMENT AND THE SICK-PROFILING!!!))),...

AND...

(((SINCE I CAN'T EVEN buy no birthday - OR - no bangin' crab cakes!!!))),...

Well...

(((I KNOW he read MY lips - WHEN - I called the cop, A: "FUCKING FLAKE"!!!)))

I'm popular,
I said, I'm popular,
(NOT what you may think!),
But on the tip you ain't NEVER heard!,

Well, well, well,
To the motherfuckin' well!,
MY FIRST BOOK,
GOT "Y'ALL" SHOOK!!!,

"Those" that been and be on some "other shit",
Be it, "they" got jammed-up,
AND NOW tryna' "work down" THEIR charges - on some "false reports" bullshit!,
Be it, "those" that been and be on some "shitty-shit"!,
AND NOW "they" shittin' themselves,
'CAUSE MY FIRST BOOK GAVE "THEM" A "LIVER HIT"!!!,
AND SO - NOW I'm EVEN MORE "popular"!,
'CAUSE "they" afraid I'm gonna "live out" those fictional words!,

I'm popular,
I said, I'm popular,
(NOT what you may think!),
But on the tip you ain't NEVER heard!,

Well, well, well,
To the motherfuckin' well!,
MY FIRST BOOK,
GOT "Y'ALL" SHOOK!!!,

"THEM": "LET'S FOLLOW THIS NIGGER!!!",
"HE'S GOT TO BE UP TO NO GOOD,
WE FIGURED!!!",
"CLEARLY, HE WROTE SOME SHIT,

WE CAN ARREST HIM ON!!!",
ME: "NOPE!!! Y'ALL COULDN'T BE MORE WRONG!!!
NOOOOOW,...EAT MY ASS MUTHAFUCKAS!!!,
AAAAAAND,...SLOB ON MY DONG!!!",

I'M POPULAR!!!,
I SAID, I'M POPULAR!!!,
(((NOT WHAT YOU MAY THINK!!!))),
BUT ON THE TIP THAT YOU (((NOW))) HEARD!!!

BI-POLAR SOLDIER

I don't give a rat's ass,
Or a lovely mother fuck,
Catch me on a bad day?,
And you're getting fucking snuck!,

And I'll spit in your face,
TO get YOU to push your luck,
AND when you wake up??,
Get the number of that truck!,

Nice on some days,
And,...worse on the next,
Don't nothin' piss me off more,
Than WHEN a motherfucker test!,

And that's a terrifying time,
And to that - I MUST confess,
((('Cause my actions surpass my thoughts))),
I don't know WHAT I'm doing next!,

Oh, Good God!,
Why is my mind this way?,
Nice one minute,
And,...the next crazy!,

Don't fuck with me,
'Cause I don't play,
And it DON'T take much,
For me to have a bad day!,

Last of all,...
I'm paranoid but not of y'all,

You know what I mean?,
(Flowers By Irene;)

EVERYDAY, ALL DAY

Everyday, all day...

Beard twisted-up,
Face tatted-up,
Head dreaded-up,
Six-Foot-Four,
And muscled-up,
Raider Nation,
Buffalo Soldier,
Black Panther,
Pimp,
Biker,
I ain't playin' dress-up,
I get dressed-up,
To get my money-up,
I rep the struggle on-up,
I rep the Nation from -
sun-up to sun-up,
(I'm talkin' straight-up -
"Black Heart - Silver Blood"!),
And for whatever may come-up?,
(Beez dat as it may!),
I stayz ready everyday, all day,
'Cause sometimes it beez like dat,
(And,...sometimes it beez dat way!),
So from my feet on-up -
(In thee event -
I gotsta' knuckle-up!),
I'm dressed like money -
and for battle,

I'm battle-ready,
(You damn right baby!),
And on dat -
there ain't no maybeez!,
Sun-up to sun-up -
Everyday -
Sun-up to sun-up -
I beez dat way -
Laptop -
All day -
Stayz-up -
All day -
Sun-up to sun-up -
(Dats how it stayz!) -
Sun-up to sun-up -
I beez on my grind-up -
(Dats how I stayz!) -
Sun-up to sun-up -
Livin' life my way -
Sun-up to sun-up -
Livin' life my way -
Sun-up to sun-up -
Livin' life my way -
Sun-up to sun-up -
Everyday, all day!

HE THOAD

That boy thoad,
He don't wear our type of clothes,
He listens to Rock n' Roll,
Y'all crabs in a barrel,
That shit is old,
Don't be held down,
'Cause they will hold,
Eat my ass,
Fuck your soul,
Peep your comings 'n goes,
Peep your clothes,
Then slit your throat,
You Got-Damn Right,
That boy is thoad!

FENTANYL PATCHES

Chewing on fentanyl patches,
Scars on my back from fingernail scratches,
Bad bitches I'm smashin',
Fuck the cops you'll never find my stashes,
Smoking on only the finest of hashes,

Hands quick like Cassius,
My left hand stings,
My right hand bashes,
My rings cause gashes,
Fuck your face up like fatal car crashes,

Evil like a facist,
Fuck the world and the masses,
Fuck the doors I'm kickin' in the latches,
4th and Goal, I'm running, no passes,
AND I got a bad temper LIKE Cash's!,
Wild walker,
Walkin',
Wildin',

Walked on the side of the wild,
With TWO clinched fists!!,

DIDN'T give a fuck IF I died!,
Ain't no comin' back from that,
I survived all that,

But...

To that,
In my mind,
Still I'm attatched.

BATTLE SCARS

Battle scars,
I come with a whirlwind AND a warning!,
And I'ma beez like that,
From late at night,
'Til early in the morning,

Lady killer,
Killin' ladies with my charm and,
I'm battle-hardened,
From Hell's Kitchen,
To Eden's Garden,

If you think I'm worth the risk?,
I dare you to take the chance!,
Come enter MY WORLD,
Of charm and romance,

Battle scars,
I come with a whirlwind AND a warning!,
And I'ma beez like that,
From late at night,
'Til early in the morning,

I'm gone to meet my Maker,
And ask Him why,
He fucked me up so bad?,
Been fucked up,
Ever since I lost my Dad,

Suicide is always on my mind,
Ever since I was a little guy,
After meth, coke is like eating cold fries,

Just a big waste of money,
And a big waste of time!,

I flew with an eagle,
And been to the Spirit World,
And I'm held hostage on YOUR planet,
Because of my little girl,

Battle scars,
I come with a whirlwind AND a warning!,
And I'ma beez like that,
From late at night,
'Til early in the morning,

I stay in the backroads,
And stay in the shadows,
You'll never hear me coming in my boots,
I stay light on my toes,

Creeping on my foes,
Line of meth up my nose,
Might hit the "Rock Ninja" technique,
I learned in the dojos,

I slip in and out of town like consciousness,
Wear all black like a ninja and leave no fingerprints,
Silent like the wind through a chain-link fence,
Then disappear like smoke from Nigerian incense,...

Battle scars,
I come with a whirlwind AND a warning!,
And I'ma beez like that,
From late at night,
'Til early in the morning,

And this won't be the first time,
I had a standoff with the cops,
SWAT Team rifle scopes in the dark,
Lookin' like I'm fightin' 8 cyclops,

I'm in the cop's dreams,
(As, it seems!),
They sent the SWAT Team,
They wasn't ready for me,

"Go home to your wives,
and your daughters!",
(THIS might turn,
Into a slaughter!),

(Think what you want,
Your thoughts are,
The bridge's passing water),...

Got lit up,
With rubber bullets, tasers, and sin!!!,
I said,
"I'm the realest YOU EVER met!!!",
THEY said,...
"Hit 'em AGAIN!!!",

Battle scars,
I come with a whirlwind AND a warning!,
And I'ma beez like that,
From late at night,
'Til early in the morning,

Church bells make my eyes swell,
'Cause I'm going to Hell,

For not living well,

May I find the peace in death,...
That I could not find in life,...

And these damn church bells,
Make my eyes swell,
'Cause, I know, I'm not livin' right!,

But I'm straight out the Bible,
Revelation 9:6,
And my dirty little whore in a vile,

And you never see me smile,
Ain't trying to be hard,
But my heart's been dead for a while,

Battle scars,
I come with a whirlwind AND a warning!,
But I'll love you all night,
'Til early in the morning,

Lady killer,
Killin' ladies with my charm and,
I'm battle-hardened,
From Hell's Kitchen,
To Eden's Garden,

If you think I'm worth the risk?,
I DARE YOU to take the chance!,
Come enter MY WORLD,
Of charm and romance.

MADMAN

The car is idling,
But his mind is not,
The madman sits there doin' what he do,
Peeping the whole parking lot,

Staring straight ahead,
Into blackness.
Into nothing.
This madman stares at nothing,
Prepping his eyes to be staring at something,

Staring straight ahead,
The madman begins to see,
The outline of the back door,
Night vision setting in,
This is the shit he lives for,

Beginning to get a lay of the land,
The madman begins by counting shadows,
Could once barely see his own hand,
If the count is off,
HE KNOWS that he's being followed,

Sitting there in silence,
With windows down,
Listening for what you don't listen for,
THAT'S the madman's sound,

Staring at the cars parked in the lot,
Until he gets that image ingrained in his mind,
Then he looks away,
Then he lays that image ingrained in his mad-brain,

Back over the scene like a template,
This madman peeps the slightest differences,
Each and every time,

Then he'll peep the whole scene,
From any object casting reflections,
Peeping differences and motions,
AS forms of detections,

That's right!,
HE'S a mother fuckin' madman!,
YOU in trouble if he knows that you're there!,

That's right!!,
HE'S A mother fuckin' MADMAN!!,
AND he don't give a fuck if YOU care!!.

BLIND MAN'S TOUCH

The view one perceives,
Upon the approach of me,
Is that of a subject,
Unmoved and unmoving,

I don't blink.
My eyes stay fixed on those,
Making thee approach,
Focused.
I focus my depth of field,

Conserving energy,
While peeping the movements,
I visualize my movements,
If to be made,
With no conservation,

I calculate in motionless-style,
My own first move,
And/Or counter-move,

And thus...

Essentially,
The irrelevancy,
Of any moves other than my own.

An artist painting a portrait,
On canvas with oil paint,
Reveals the artist's true depth perception in depth,
Of the subject in depth,

Therefore...

A blind man's touch,
Of a print,
Of my self-portrait,
On canvas in oil,
Is my facial expression.

Paranoid of trust,
With the instilled general feeling,
That today just may be a good day,
To bust someone dead in their face,
Because that's what they need,
I get out the bed ready for moments like these,

For(You See)...

This is my life on the Serengeti,
This is my life of self-preservation,
This is how I earned the gray hairs in my twisted beard,
This is my life in your world.

CROSS

BEING BORN

Right around dawn...

I am violently awoken,
Suffering from a massive seizure,
Thrown awake,
From seconds earlier,
Lying flat on my back,
At the base of two red faded,
Chipped, flaking, and cracked,
Arched doors,
Early in the morn,
Upon an old abandoned,
Church platform,

On my back,
What I find,...
I'M under attack!,
My arms to my sides,
Slightly bent at the elbows,
(What the fuck AM I in for???),
(((ONLY God knows!))),
My head laid to my side,
Resting on its left,...

With thoughts on the inside,...

"I may NOT HAVE much time left!",...

I hop up off the platform, time,...and again,...

As...

I have no control over my body,...

As...

My body and life seizes up,...

It's the ending of my life!,
A life,...lived on the edge,...

AND...

"I bet NOT one,
WON'T GIVE a single fuck!",

For(you see!)...

The violent seizure of my body,
MOVES ME like a see-saw,
In the direct path,
(((Of straight-line heavy storm winds!!!))),

AND...

It's IMPOSSIBLE to fight!,
Got me flopping FOR life!,
Like the impending death of a fish,...
I'M being reeled in!,

And, I think to myself,...

"I've tried it,
but, this time,
simple and plain,
I think, I'm really dying!",

And(It AIN'T nothin' more than!)...

A violent ending...TO a life...that was FAR FROM a game!

And, I think to myself...

"Just kick your right leg,
a couple of times,
two or three kicks should be enough,
to wake yourself up.",

(In my mind surmises)...

AS...

I am FULLY aware,
That I was just awakened,
BY this violent seizure!,

I am FULLY aware,
Continually VIOLENTLY shaken,
I am NOT in control!!,

I am FULLY aware,
Who's blood stains I'VE SEEN,
MAY BE possessing me!!!,

I am FULLY aware,
The shadowy figures that HAVE resided,
IN the corners of my eyes,
MAY HAVE COME for my soul!!!!,

AND SO...

Managing to kick my right foot three times,
By bending my right knee,
And then lunging my foot forward,
Gives me some sense of confidence,
With this new found data,
That I still have some say-so of some sorts!,

On how I move,
Which proves,
Which provides,
Me a slim sliver of hope,
That I'll be able to wake myself up,

Although this is something unlike,
I have ever experienced before,
And I know this ain't good,
That, yet, and perhaps,
Things aren't as bad as they seem,
That feeling,
That slight glimmer of hope,
Is fleeting,

That feeling,
That slight glimmer of help,
Quickly passes from me,

That feeling,
Of only feeling,
The heel of my right foot scoot,

That feeling,
Of barely skimming the surface,
With my right cowboy boot,

That feeling,
Of NOW realizing!,
That,...THAT WAS my best AND ONLY attempt!,

That feeling,
OF KNOWING,
THAT WASN'T ENOUGH!!!,

That feeling,
OF KNOWING,
I CAN'T wake myself up!,

That feeling,
OF TO DO SO,
I AM exempt!,

FOR(YOU SEE!)...

I HAVE BEEN rendered free,
OF the ability,
To open my eyes and sit up!!,

And so...

My eyes ARE STILL closed!!,

As...

They have been this WHOLE time!!,

AND...

(I'm STILL TRYING to compute IN my mind!)...

As(TO WHY?!?)...

Is it,
THAT I,
Could ONLY feel the bottom,
Skim the surface of THAT platform,
WITH THIS RIGHT BOOT HEEL OF MINE?!?,

Hmm...

(Could it be that I am levitating???)...

'Cause...

(IF so!)...

NORMALLY, I'm one, that WOULD SO BE,
Into THAT, SORT OF thing!!!,
ALWAYS knew that I was different!,
And one, that had some shit about him!,

Hmm...

Maybe one day,
I'll look back and say,...

"I levitated! THAT SHIT was cool!",...

HOWEVER...

(AS, for NOW!)...

"Of THIS, I'VE had enough!,
I JUST WANT TO wake myself up!!",...

Once feeling...

The platform strike between my shoulder blades,
AND THEN ONLY THE BACKS OF MY HEELS,
AS my heels and my blades would ALTERNATE,...
AS CONTACT WITH THE CHURCH PLATFORM WAS MADE!!!,...

'CAUSE...

That's how I WAS so,
BEING VIOLENTLY THROWN!!!,

And(NOW)...

I feel nothing.

The seizure,
(That lasted ONLY but a minute!),
But,...TRUST ME!!!,
QUITE LONG ENOUGH,
IF YOU'RE THE ONE,
GOING THROUGH THAT SHIT!!!,
Has ended.

THOUGH...

NOT because,
I HAD THE power,
TO MAKE IT stop!,...

(No! No! No!)

RATHER...

IT stopped,
Just because,
IT STOPPED tossing me!,

And(NOW!)...

I CAN'T feel,
MY body lying flat,
On my back,
Not MY back,
Not MY legs,
Not the backs,
Of MY heels!!,

Nor...

MY arms to MY sides,
Slightly bent at the elbows,

Nor...

MY head laid to MY left,
Lying on its left side,

AND SO...

(I know WHAT I gotta do!)...

“Let me,...lift up my head,
and,...open my eyes,
and,...see if anyone can see me,
and,...are able to tell,...
WHAT the hell,...I’M going through!?!”,

(I thought to myself!)...

THOUGH...

(NOT necessarily TO help!)...

FOR(YOU SEE!!!)...

(I DON’T expect NO ONE to help!)...

‘CAUSE...

(THAT’S HOW people ARE in your moment OF need!)...

EVEN(SO!)...

I JUST want to know,
If ANYONE ELSE knows,
WHAT I’M going through!,

OR...

(IF I’M just lying here)...

Going through it alone.

And so...

I lift up my head off the platform,
And I open my eyes,
And upon turning my head to my right,
The grainy hazy blue image,
Of what I see,
(Of no one there OF importance!),
Comes to me AS no surprise!,
And so(essentially!)...

WHAT I have felt,
And HAVE KNOWN all along,
It's just, me,
It's just,...ALWAYS been me!,

For(YOU see!)...

Other than, me?,
The ONLY one,
That HAS MY back,
(Early in THIS morn!),
In the most realist moment in time,
IN MY ENTIRE LIFE,...
IS this old abandoned church platform!!!,

And so...

In turn,
I find myself going,
FROM A novice,
TO AN intern!,

AS...

It's now MY turn!,

WITH ALL hope buried,
Might as well get to working,
On BEING interned!,

AS...

I turn,
My head back to my left,
And close my eyes,
And lower the back of my head,
To once again,
Be resting,
On my ol' church platform,

AS(Then!)...

ONCE AGAIN...

My head rolls to my left.
And,...once again...

All alone.

With the side of my face,
On its left side rests,
Against my old abandoned church platform,
Getting ready for this interment death!,...

But(THEN!)...

Something...

Comes across me!

SOMETHING...

THAT I'm NOW realizing!!!

AS...

I'M lying there!,
IN the darkness OF MY body!,

Something...

(((IS dawning on me!)))

On the dawn of this day in the morning,...

I DIDN'T lift up my head!,
I DIDN'T open my eyes!!,
I DIDN'T turn my head to the right!,
(TO SEE what I knew,
what I ALREADY KNEW,
I would find!),

(THAT BEING!!!)...

IF I WERE to see,
ANYBODY there WITH me?,
And THEY KNEW,
WHAT I was going through??,...

Well...

THEY WERE probably playing it off like,
They had NOOOOOO idea,
At all IN MY MOMENT,
OF THE MOST REAL!!!,

JUST TO...

Let me go through it.

Just to...

LET ME go through it BY MYSELF.

JUST SO...

I would die.

But(YET!)...And(BUT STILL!!)...

WHAT just (((dawned))) ON ME?...(((WAS JUST AS REAL!!!)))...

"I saw that grainy hazy,
blue scene of nobody, (there),
THROUGH the right side of my head!!!",...

(I thought to myself!)...

AS...

I'M STILL completely AND FULLY aware!,
OF MY consciousness, thought, and sight!!!,
(((JUST AS YOU have RIGHT NOW,
AT this VERY MOMENT in time!!!))),...

THOUGH...

Having had no fear, no panic,
Or not even having,
A sense of wanting,
Someone TO COME help me,
OR the feeling OF,
NOT WANTING to die,
(This ENTIRE time!),

For(You see!)...

This NEW found realization OF KNOWING,
I just saw the church platform,
AND the arched entrance,
Of the walls its enclosing,

OUT THE RIGHT SIDE of my head!,
WITHOUT OPENING my eyes!!,
Kick starts my heart to flutter,
LIKE A BILLION butterflies!!!!!!,

But(Yet)...And(BUT STILL!!!)...

WITH MY FACE STILL lying on the platform,
STILL WITH IT JUST ON my left side!,
STILL WITH my arms TO MY sides,
At the elbows slightly bent,...

I'm not feeling ANY of it!

(NOR am I feeling!)...

THAT...

THIS JUST MAY BE,
A good time FOR ME,...TO repent!!!,

'Cause...

With me STILL,...

Lying ON the platform...

With me STILL,...

Flat ON my back,...

(((I'M NOT FEELING ANY OF THAT!!!)))

AS...

I lie there,
Lying there,
IN the empty shell of MY body,
IN MY oblivion OF black!,...

AS...

I think to myself...
"I CAN'T feel my body!,
BUT, I know, that I'm lying here!,
I feel like,...I'm down in myself,...
within myself.,
I feel like,...my body IS whole.,
BUT,...I feel like,...my body,
is an empty hollow shell.",...

EVEN SO...

Those few seconds of thought...(((ALL THE WAY THROUGH)))...

My heart IS STILL fluttering,
LIKE A BILLION butterflies!!!!!!,
(((Almost ticklish is the feeling!))),
Of what I compare it to!,

And...

(((It's the ONLY THING that I CAN feel!)))

And(THEN)...

My heart begins,
To knock around in my chest,
Like it's bouncing and tumbling,
Off of EVERY rib!,...

Lying there...

Motionless.
In my black oblivion.
I am fully aware,
That my heart's ricocheting,

Is only being contained,
BY rib cage AND sternum!!,

And(Yet!)...Even(WITH THAT!!)...

The INTERIOR side,
OF MY rib cage and sternum,
AS MY HEART tumbles and ricochets,
IN A clockwise motion,...
I CAN'T FEEL the impact!!,

BUT(YET)...AND(BUT STILL!!)...

WITH consciousness AND thought!!,
I am FULLY aware!,
That I'm continually lying there!!,

AS...
(I can ONLY visualize)...

As...

(I'm TRYING to imagine)...(((WHAT it's looking like INSIDE!!!)))...

AND...

What I see is what I guess,
It's looking like inside my chest,
My heart is now a clockwise-knuckleball,
Tumbling around and around and around again,
Like the damage done by a bowling ball,
My heart is now the tumbling pins,

But(Yet)...And(BUT STILL!!!)...

There is no fear.
There is no panic.
And I feel no pain.

As...

I'm lying there...

In my black oblivion,
Down in myself,
Within myself,

As...

I think to myself...

"I'm having a heart attack, I'm dying."

As...

I think to myself...

"One LAST time of trying!"

AS...

I think to myself...

"Let me,...lift my head up again,
and,...turn it to the right,
and,...open my eyes,
and,...just take one more,
LAST look around to be sure,
if there's anyone there,
that knows,...what's going down,
and knows,...what I'm going through?,
('cause, THIS is some shit TO BE going through!),
and, if so,...if there's anyone there,...that cares?",

And...(DON'T YOU KNOW!!!)...

UPON seeing...

THEE. EXACT. SAME. Blue image. OF grainy haze!,...

(I know that there's nobody there!)

And, I think to myself...

"Look. At. THIS. Shit! ...Certainly,...nobody,...THAT cares!"

And, I think to myself...

"IF anyone were there THIS TIME??,
They would just play it off,
LIKE they had NOOOOOO idea!",

JUST...

"To let me go through it myself!"

Just...

"To let me go through it BY MYSELF!"

Just...

"TO LET ME die!"

And so...

I turn my head back to the left,
Against the church platform,
I lower the back of my head to rest,

And(then)...

I close my eyes.

As...

My head slowly and gently...rolls to my left.

Coming to a stop.
My face lying on its left,
Where it gently,...
Comes to a rest.

And so...

Lying there...

Flat on my back,
With my arms to my sides,
Slightly bent at the elbows,
With my head laid to my left,
With my eyes closed,
In my black oblivion,
Down in myself,
Down in my oblivion of black,
Within myself,
UNABLE to feel myself,
WHILE my heart STILL continues,
To ricochet as it tumbles,
(The ONLY THING I can feel!),
Imagining how it MUST look!,
(That of MY heart!),...
BOUNCING THE FUCK AROUND,
INSIDE OF MY CHEST!!!

Knowing...

(UPON taking that last look!)...

Knowing...

((That no one is there who cares!!))...

KNOWING...

(((THAT NO ONE KNOWS WHAT'S GOING ON!!!)))...

AND KNOWING...

(With that LAST look!)...

Coming TO THE realization,...
ONCE AGAIN!!!,
THAT I SAW that grainy hazy blue image,...
(((THROUGH the right side of MY head!!!))),

AND SO...

(((IN MY MOMENT OF TRUTH!!!)))...

Harikari-style of MY OWN sword,
IF I WERE TO pray to the Lord!,

THOUGH...

Did I ask,...God,...FOR forgiveness?,
Did I ask,...The Lord,...TO save me?,...

(((Are YOU motherfuckin' crazy?!?)))

FOR(YOU SEE!)...

I ALWAYS thought something else,...was out there!,
Something,...much larger and greater THAN myself!

However...

(I NEVER REALLY believed!)

FOR(YOU SEE!!)...

(I NEVER REALLY had proof!!)

AND SO...

TO BEG for forgiveness now??,
I KNEW I'D BE a hypocrite!!!,...

(((IN MY MOMENT OF TRUTH!!!)))

AND SO...

(((AT MY moment OF truth!!!)))...

I say to myself...
"I'm having a heart attack,
I'm dying.
Fuck it!
I'm just going to relax,
and let it happen."

(((JUST THINK ABOUT THAT SHIT FOR A MINUTE!!!)))...

'Cause...

(AS, SOON AS, I said that?)...

I felt my heart stop!

And...

I could not feel a thing.

OTHER THAN...

The feeling,
That I was down IN myself,
WITHIN myself,
Within the black oblivion,
OF MY lifeless earthly shell,...

(My former self).

Then...

I feel and hear a loud “THUD”!

(Right in the middle of my breastplate!)

AS(IF)...

Something knocked on my chest one time.

For(You See!)...

THIS ENTIRE time,

I COULDN’T HEAR SHIT!!!,

(OTHER THAN ONE THING!)

AND...

THAT loud “THUD!”,
IS WHAT it was!

AND...

Up UNTIL that time,
I DIDN’T EVEN realize,
That I couldn’t even hear the sounds,
IN MY chest,
That WAS made,
(((AS MY HEART RICOCHETED))),
AND tumbled around!,

And, I think to myself...

“That I had read parts,
of the Bible enough,
to remember THIS part:
If I knock and you hear,
and answer the knock,

that I will come into you,
and with you sup."

And so...

Down in myself,
WITHIN myself,
Within the black oblivion,
OF MYSELF,...

I think to myself...

"I never really knew,...exactly what that meant."

BUT...

"Maybe,...I just heard that knock?"

And(Then!)...

(This feeling comes over me!)...

This super-relaxed feeling,
More relaxed than I had,
EVER felt EVER before!,

(((More relaxed than I had EXPECTED to feel!!!)))...

WHEN...

I told myself,
DOWN IN myself,
WITHIN myself,
In THE blackness,
OF MY shell,...

"Just to relax."

And...

"LET death happen!"

For(you see)...

This was ME letting go.

(NO LONGER trying)...(to hold onto life!)...

But(THEN!!!)...

THIS FEELING,
This INCREDIBLE feeling,
Started in my chest,
And it WENT UP my spine,
And THROUGH my neck,
And THEN into my head,
And then shot back down INTO my legs,
AND DOWN into my feet,
MAKING this super-relax feeling,
(((ENCOMPASSING MY WHOLE BODY COMPLETE!!!))),

(And I'm lying there)...

Thinking to myself...

"The best that anyone has ever felt,
in their WHOLE ENTIRE life,
be it from sex,
or from drugs,
or even from falling in love,
or from seeing their first child born.
Compared to THIS feeling?
IT WOULDN'T EVEN BE,...a molecule,...
(((((((In ALL seven seas!!!!!!!)))))))"

(And I'M lying there!)...

WITH my eyes closed,
FLAT on my back!,
WITH MY arms by my sides!!,
With MY elbows slightly bent,
AND WITH the left side of my face,
Resting gently AGAINST,
THE OLD ABANDONED CHURCH PLATFORM,
Made of white stone,

(AND I'M LYING THERE!!)...

RIGHT THERE...

AT the base,
OF arched church doors,
Suffering FROM old chipped faded red paint!,
INSIDE OF MY black oblivion,
OF my former earthly self!,
DOWN IN my empty HOLLOW shell,
DOWN IN myself,
WITHIN myself,

AS I...

BEGIN to feel myself,
LEAVE myself,
(((And PULL DOWN))),...
OUT OF myself!,

RIGHT THERE...

(IN the middle OF my back!)...

(((WITH THAT INCREDIBLE FEELING)))...gone.

I CAN NOT FEEL MY BODY,

Lying ON the platform!,

But...

RIGHT THERE...

(RIGHT IN the middle of MY back!)...

I feel a slight pressure,
Like the feeling of a single drop of water,
Suspended from a faucet,...

That finally gives way.

AND...

(((THAT'S WHAT I FEEL!!!)))

AS...

(((I LEAVE MYSELF!!!)))

(RIGHT IN the middle of my back!)...

Lowering down...

OUT OF myself!

Lowering slowly down...

OUT OF myself!

Lowering down...

INTO a oblivion of black!

And(YET!)...

I CAN SEE myself!,
ABOVE myself!,

And(IN ADDITION TO THAT!!)...

I can NOW see,
(A small circular ripple)),
Is WHAT it APPEARS to be!,

(RIGHT IN the middle of my back!))...

WHERE it was that I finally,...
PULLED DOWN OUT OF MY BODY!!!,

Lowering, down, down, down,...

Into THIS black oblivion,
I can see MY body above!,

AS I...

Keep lowering down,...

(AND I'M lying there!)...

FLAT ON MY BACK!,
FLOATING on my back!,
Floating ON the surface,
OF THIS oblivion OF black!,

The SAME oblivion,
To take me,
IT'S continuing!,...

WITH my head laid to the left side,
WITH my arms by my sides!!,
Slightly bent at the elbows,...

AS...

I CAN SEE myself positioned,
(JUST LIKE THAT!),

Floating there!,
(JUST LIKE THAT!),
Floating on the surface,
Of the black oblivion,...

And(As I look)...(I SEE!!)...

(RIGHT IN the middle of my back!)...

WITH WHAT APPEARS TO BE,
(A black circular ripple)),
((GROWING)))...AND...((((SPREADING OUT))))))))))),...

((((((((((((((((((RIGHT IN THE MIDDLE OF MY
BACK!!!))))))))))))))))...

WHERE I pulled down out!

AS(IF)...

A single small pebble,
Were tossed into a still pond,
Black oblivion waters so calm,...

Lowering down, down, down,...

(I'm ALMOST gone!)...

WITH MY BODY FLOATING ABOVE,
ATOP of this black ripple IN my sight!!,

AND(I'M)...

Lowering, down, down, down,...

UNTIL my body ABOVE,
IS out of sight!!,

Lowering down, down, down,...

There is no sound.
Nor am I in fear,...

BUT...

I still have consciousness,
Thought and sight,
(((Just as YOU have right now,
At this very moment!!!))),

The ONLY difference is,...
I CAN NOT hear!!,

And, I think to myself!...

"That black ripple above,
like I'm in black waters,
the waters of death,
am I lowering down into the river Styx?,
Will the boatman come for me?,
Or will it be the Grim Reaper?",

(I don't know!)

BUT...

(What I DO know!!)...

I just keep getting slowly lowered down, down, down,...

INTO this black oblivion!,
WITH NO END TO THIS IN SIGHT!!,
WITH NO DEEP END TO THIS BLACK OBLIVION,
WITH ALL OF IT DEEPER!!!,

And then,...just then...

(Out of nowhere!)

Though...

(NOT as a shock!)

It FELT like two hands just came,
From far back wayback,
From the horizon's grave,
In the middle of my back,
Both hands gently placed,...

Though...

(SOMEWHAT of a shock!)

AS...

I'm gently lowered to a stop.

Looking around,
The blackest I've ever seen,
Above, to the sides, and below,
Just the oblivion of a black screen!,

No more lowering down, down, down.

And, I think to myself...

"Well, this is pretty much what,
I thought death would be like.",...

"Though, blacker of an oblivion,
THAN I thought it would be!",...

"Only thing is,...
I didn't think,...
I'D EVEN KNOW,...

I'd be here!",...

"I guess,...this is where,...I'll forever be.",...

And then...

Taking another look around,
Of my eternal home,
I actually chuckle to myself,...

"Well, at least I'm alone!"

And then,...JUST THEN...

That incredible feeling...(((CAME BACK!!!)))...

It started in my heart,
And once again,
Traveled up my spine and,
Into my head and,
(((I CAN FEEL ALL THIS!!!))),
(((THIS incredible feeling!!!))),
AS it shoots back down through my chest,
Into my legs and,
Into my arms and,
I feel like I'm lying flat on my back,
In this black oblivion of death,
Being gently held by two hands,...

This feeling...

I think to myself...
"IS the greatest feeling in the world!,
I've never felt anything like this!,
It feels like,...
pure love,...

and comfort,...
and acceptance!,
I feel like,...
I'm being loved,...
just because,...
I'm me."
And then,...just like that...

I'M LIFTED UP INTO THE LIGHT!!!!!!!

(It felt like I shot up at a 45 degree angle!)...

And then...there I was...

UP IN THE LIGHT!!!!!!!

NOTHING grainy or hazy,
About THIS light!!!!!!!,
EVERYTHING was full of vivid colors!!!!!!!,
And EVERYTHING was bright!!!!!!!,
As I'm looking down on myself,
FROM UP ABOVE!!!!!!!,...

At times...

I could see the whole neighborhood,
Could see for miles,
Every tree,
The roofs of houses,
And myself lying there,
Graveyard and steeple and all,
As I lie there on the platform,
Flat on my back,
With my head laid to the left,
With my arms down by my sides,

Slightly bent at the elbows,
Died on the platform,
Of my old abandoned church,
And in comparison,...
I KNOW I WAS SHOWN,
A VALUABLE LESSON!!!,
Eternal death in that black oblivion,
Was SO MUCH worse!,

No longer down in myself,...
Within myself,...

BUT...

UP IN THE BRIGHT BLUE BEAUTIFUL SKY!!!

At times...
It would appear that I'm,
Looking down on myself,
Through a tunnel,
Black on all sides,
Looking down at myself,
FROM WAY UP HIGH!!!!!!!,

But(At ALL times!)...

I can CLEARLY see myself,
(((((((IN a circle of brightness))))))),
Like I'm looking at himself,
(((((((THROUGH a tunnel of DARKNESS))))))),

And(ALL the while!)...

I just keep looking around!,
FROM WAY UP HIGH IN THE LIGHT!!!!!!!,
And seeing MYSELF,

WHILE looking down!,

WHILE, I'm thinking to myself!...

"That I felt like I was a ball of light,
WITH thought AND sight!!!",

And so...

(Having NEVER felt OR seen ANYTHING like THIS before!)...

I think to himself,...

"Am I an orb?"

With complete consciousness,
With complete thought,
And with complete sight,
(((JUST AS YOU HAVE RIGHT NOW,
AT THIS VERY MOMENT!!!))),...

I say to myself,...(((in COMPLETE amazement!!!)))...

"I can't believe,
there's really a God!,
I can't believe,
there's really a Heaven!,
I can't believe,
God thought enough of,
a little piece of shit like me,
to bring me up to Heaven,
and have me up here with Him,
UP IN THE LIGHT!!!!!!!,
AND IN THE BRIGHT BLUE!!!!!!!,
I can't believe,...
ALL those things,...

IN the Bible,...
ARE true!!!!!!!"

And as I'm looking at myself,...

FROM WAY UP HIGH!!!!!!!,
From time to time,
Right across my vision,
Something white would travel by,...

And, I'd say to myself...

"Was that a cloud?,
Am I a cloud?,
Am I up,...
In THE sky??"

And, I'm feeling as though...

I'm a ball of light,
WITH thought AND sight,...

And(ALTHOUGH!)...

I DON'T see anyone else,
With me way up in the sky,...

I DON'T feel as though I'M alone!,

FOR...

(((I can feel it!))),
(((I can SENSE it!!))),
(((I can feel the presence!!!))),
(((Of somebody else!!!!)))))))))))),
(((Someone FAR GREATER!!!!!!!))))))),...than myself.

And, I put thought to whom that person might be?...

"I'm either here with Jesus,
The Virgin Mary,
or maybe it's my Dad.",

('Cause, my Dad passed many years back)

HMM...

"MAYBE, by Dad,
I'm thinking and saying,...
Father God?",...

As...

I hover there,...

(((Feeling like a ball of light))),
(((WITH thought AND sight))),

WITH thought and sight,...

(((JUST AS YOU HAVE RIGHT NOW!!!)))

Believe it or not?...(it's really not so odd!)

Hovering...

Way up there in the sky,
The bright blue sky of morning,
With what must be a cloud passing,
Through my vision on occassion,
Seeing myself,
Looking down on myself,
FROM WAY UP HIGH!!!!!!!,

And, thinking to myself...

"I don't know if this is Heaven?,

I might actually...be in Heaven.,
Because,...nothing...could feel better than this."

And then,.. just after that...

I get this feeling,
The feeling that from where I was,
The ball of light within the presense,
(((((((Of ONE GREATER than myself))))))),
I felt that from there,
I was supposed to go,
Somewhere else,...

And so...

I decide to look behind,
And way out in the distance,
In the distance of the blue morning horizon,
(((((((I SEE A BEAMING GOLD CIRCULAR LIGHT))))))),
And I'm feeling AS THOUGH,
From here,...THAT'S WHERE I was supposed to go!,...
(((((((To go WITH the presense GREATER)))))))...than myself.

And, I think to myself...

"If the sun rises in the east,
and I'm looking west,
then what is that light?,
Like they always say,
'Go towards the light!',
And I'm getting that feeling too!,
Upon seeing a light,
that I feel as though,
that's where I'm supposed to go!"

AND SO...

I turn back around,
And look down,
On myself lying there,
On the platform,
And I can see the whole neighborhood,
Rooftops, trees and all,
And still feeling this incredible feeling,
Of pure comfort and pure love,

And then...

I look back at that light,...

And then...

I look back down on myself lying there,...

And, I say to myself...

"This is great!
I get to feel like (((((((THIS))))))),
for ALL of (((((((eternity?))))))),
I WANT TO STAY!!!!!!!
I DON'T want to go back!,
I DON'T want to go back down there!,
...I might not make it back up here."

And(with that)...

MY vision is that of myself,
(((((((Looking through a tunnel at myself))))))),
And I can see myself clearly,
(((((((But it's all black on all sides))))))),

And, I'M PLEADING as I say...

"No! No! No! Wait!"

AS...

(((((((I COME SHOOTING BACK DOWN THAT TUNNEL!!!!!!!)))))))

Right AT myself!,
Lying there,
Flat on my back,
On the platform,
Of my abandoned church,
WITH MY head TO the left,
Face laid TO THE side,
WITH MY arms to MY sides,
Slightly bent at the elbows,
(YOU KNOW HOW THIS GOES!!!),
Legs flat on the platform,
Not bent at the knees,
Not IN myself,
NOT DOWN WITHIN myself,...

For...

(((((((I AM UP ABOVE!!!!!!!)))))))

AS...

(((((((I'M COMING BACK DOWN THIS TUNNEL))))))),
(((((((AT A SPEED))))))),
(((((((NOT EVEN COMPREHENDIBLE!!!!!!!))))))),...

And...

BAM!!!,
I POP UP!!!,
(((((((JUST AT THE WAIST!!!))))))),

MY lifeless body once lying,

There flat ON MY back,
I sit straight up!,
(((((((Bending JUST AT the waist!!!))))))),
I came up SO fast,
(((((((Like a GIANT spring was IN my back!!!))))))),

IF...

Someone were there,
WITH ME THAT CARED!!!,
And was leaning overtop of me,
Shaking me?,

Asking me...

'Hey, Rod, are you alright?'

IF...

There were a person there,
That EVEN cared?,
The WAY I popped up,
With SO MUCH force,
(((((((JUST AT THE WAIST))))))),...

IF...

Our heads collided?,
(((((((THEY WOULD HAVE EXPLODED!!!!!!))))))),

And so...

Sitting there...

On the platform...

To myself, all I can manage to say is...

"Whoa."

Sitting there...

On the platform...

Still out flat are my legs,
With my hands by my sides,
Slightly bent at the elbows,
Holding myself in place,...

And...

I look down at my watch,
The time is 5:32am on the dot,

And(then)...

I stand up...

To check my reflection,
In an object reflecting,
And I'm reflecting,
In reflection,

And...

I'm immediately depressed that I'm back.

REMEMBRANCES OF REVERENCES

And so...

I tell her...

How there wasn't any sound,
Except for when I heard,
That single knock on my breastplate,

And...

How I felt like,
I may have already been dead,

And remembrances of...

That part of the Bible I read,

And...

Of how upon remembering that,
I was ready to meet my fate!,

And...

How I felt as though I was lying there,
Like I was inside of my empty shell,
And how I never felt that way before,
And how when I heard that knock,
I thought that was Jesus at my soul's door,

Of how there was no panic.
No pain.
And no fear.

Of how it all just felt like,

The natural process of dying,
Kinda like how a baby deer is born,
Into the world,
And doesn't know,
Anything about anything.

But...

It knows...

It has to stick close to its mother!,
And for nourishment it has to suckle!,

But...

The deer don't know.

But(SOMEHOW)...

It knows!

AND...

THAT'S just the natural process of birth!

And so...

What I felt it to be,...was the natural process of death.

And...

I explained how when I heard that knock,
I didn't ask God for forgiveness,
For my life of sin,

'Cause...

I didn't want to be a hypocrite.

But...

God still loved me.

And...

God saved me.

And...

Held me.

(((((((UP IN THE LIGHT!!!!!!!)))))))

To show me first hand,
The proof I always needed.

And(THEN)...

God sent me back!

Alighted from...(((((((THE LIGHT!!!!!!!)))))))

To LET ME live the rest of my life,
And FOR ME just TO know,
(((((((That I AM up here waiting FOR you!!!!!!!))))))),

Or...

Next time,...I'll keep you down below.

BUT...

THAT'S UP TO YOU!!!!!!!

And as I described to her,
How I felt my heart stop,
She leaned into me,
And I held her so,

And when I described to her,
(((((((THAT INCREDIBLE FEELING!!!!!!!))))))),

I began (((((((TO FEEL))))))),
And I asked her,
"Do you (((((((FEEL THAT))))))) too?",
And she replied, ((((((("Yes."))))))),
(And then right on cue!),
Out of the corner of my eye,
Right there in the living room,...
THERE WAS (((((((A BEAMING ARCH OF LIGHT!!!!!!!))))))),

Which...

(Didn't connect at the top)...

Nor...

(Did it come all the way down to the floor)...

But...
(((((((THERE IT WAS!!!!!!!)))))))

(((((((BEAUTIFUL BEAMING AND BRIGHT!!!!!!!))))))),
Like that same (((((((BRIGHT BEAUTIFUL COLOR))))))),
When I (((((((felt))))))) as though,...
I should (((((((GO TOWARDS THE LIGHT!!!!!!!))))))),

And...

When I turned my head to look...

(((((((THE ARCH)))))))...(((((((((flickered)))))...away.

And...

As I sat there holding her,
And telling her that there was nothing to fear,
And that everything was gonna be alright,...

That Arch...(((((((((((((((((((REAPPEARED!!!!!!!)))))))

BACK OUT THE CORNER OF MY EYE!!!!!!!,
(((((((THAT BRIGHT BEAUTIFUL BEAMING LIGHT!!!!!!!))))))),
(((((((THAT ARCH OF GOLD!!!!!!!))))))),...

I'll remember (((((((THAT ARCH))))))) even when I am old.

And...

As I held her,
I wanted to tell her to look,

But,

I didn't.

'Cause...

(((((((THAT ARCH)))))))...wasn't meant for her to see!

FOR...

(((((((THAT ARCH)))))))...was for her (((((((TO FEEL!!!!!!!)))))))

'Cause...

WHEN I turned my head again to see...

(((((((THE ARCH)))))))))...((FLICKERED)))))...AWAY!!!!!!!

FOR...

(((((((IT WAS MEANT TO BE FELT!!!!!!!)))))))

AND...

NOT looked at directly!

For...

God wanted it that way.

WHEN YOU'RE DYING

When you can see through your eyelids,
And through the side of your head,
That's when you're dying,

When you feel like you're inside your body,
Like your body is a shell,
That's when you're dying,

When the only thing you can feel,
Is your heart beating,
That's when you're dying,

When the only thing you can feel,
Is your heart stop,
That's when you're dying,

When you feel yourself,
Lower down out of yourself,
That's when you're dying,

When you go down into complete darkness,
But still have thought and sight - And you see your body above,
That's when you're dead.

When you feel like you're being held,
And an overwhelming feeling of love comes over you,
That's when you're saved,

When you're lifted up into the light,
And you feel nothing but peace and love and comfort,
That's when you're in Heaven...

SMOKY MOUNTAIN SUNSET (UNIVERSAL SOUL - PRELUDE)

White 3-Rail Horse Fencing,
Surrounds the grounds,
Dead center is a huge man-made pond,

BUT...

JUST WATCH that thick sticky-mud bottom,
(bless your heart!),...
YOUR ass will be gone!,

From the ranch porch,
It's picturesque,
From the white rocking chairs,
The view of the Smoky Mountain pinnacle,
IS the best!,

(AND the view changes!)

BIG BLUE way-up-high sky,
With big white fluffy clouds,
IT AMAZES!!,

(And there ain't NOTHING LIKE a Smoky Mountain sunset!)

Reds from the veil above,
Cuts through tree covered-mountains,
Cuts like,...
The sky was bled,

In the evening when the sun is goin' down,...
White and yellow lights,
Speckle the mountain ranges,

From distant towns,

Blinking red lights on towers can be seen,
And ain't nothin' to hear some "traveling" gunshots,...
(If you know WHAT I mean!),

And...

If you look close,...

And...

Know WHAT to look for,...

THEN...

(You'll KNOW what you're looking at!)

AS...

(Bright blue tiny flames accent the mountains),...

WITH(THAT!)...

"My-daddy's-daddy-taught-my-daddy!",...

And...

"I'm just keeping it in the family!",...

And...

"It AIN'T illegal 'til you put fire to that!",...

And...

"This-here what we're doin' is - JUST the family craft!",...

And...

"We ain't sellin' YOU none - 'Cause YOU MIGHT BE a rat!",...

And...

“If you ain’t kin? - YOU BETTER come WITH cash!”,...

And...

“We STILL use a camo tarp - to keep things under wraps!”,...

And...

“We up here in these mountains - WAAAAAAY in the back!”,...

And...

“Our ol’ hound dog let’s us know - IF the Sherrif is comin’ back!”,...

And...

“OUR shit is 100 Proof - Drippin’ out the tap!”,...

AND...

“Yes! - Our shit IS boobytrapped!”,...

And...

(((I’MA JUST LEAVE IT AT THAT!!!)))

‘CAUSE...

THAT’S “Our heritage” SHIT - IS GOIN’ DOWN!!!

UNIVERSAL SOUL

Over ponderings...

Overlooking the pond,
Just he and his drink,
A toad or two or three,

And...

(Some time to think)...

AND...

As he looks up from,
The drink in his glass,
To him, the night sky looks like,
(As if),...
Millions or billions of years ago in the past,...

The stars in the night sky,
WERE at some point in time,
IN a great giant palm,...

And...

SMEARED CROSS THE SKY!!!

And...

(The MORE that he looked?)...

Well...

(The more that WAS exposed!!)...

FOR...

TO HIM, (you see),
You have certain stars,
That JUST seem to be,
Far bigger than,
All the others and,
To the earth,
Far more close!,

Almost like...

IF he REALLY tried,
            HE could reach up,...

And...

PLUCK THEM OUT THE SKY!!!

And(Then)...

TO HIM,
THERE'S all of those OTHER stars!,
That they just seem to be,
Waaaaaaay-up-there-oh-so-high -
            and-oh-soooooo-VERY-far!,

And(THEN)...

TO HIM,
You have ALL OF THOSE,
Stars that look like tiny pinholes!,
The ones that SEEM TO APPEAR outta nowhere!,

(The ones that make you think)...

"Hmm,...WERE THEY ALWAYS THERE???"

(The ones that make you think)...

"Geez,...
I can't believe,
I'm EVEN ABLE to see,
all of these,
tiny specks of light,
WITH the naked eye!!",

The ones that just breakthrough,
The - upper-dark-outer-shelf - of outer space!,
The ones that make you feel at peace,
The ones that give you a sense of grace,

The ones far more precious than gold,
The ones like little tiny lights of pinholes,
The ones that make one feel,
(As if),...
The Universe is showing YOU its soul.

FOR, WHEN (PRELUDE)

And so...

He opens up his black and white composition book,
Sitting there, thinking of what to write,...
And as he does he FEELS as though,
He is being watched,...FROM THE SKY!!!,

As he looks up there HE SEES,...
A gigantic face in a gigantic cloud!,
As he thinks to himself,
"Could this,...REALLY be??? ,

He keeps looking up at that gigantic cloud,
BEGINNING TO BELIEVE,
There certainly APPEARS to be, (yes!),
There's REALLY a gigantic face,
IN that gigantic cloud,
More so, than, there is not!,

'CAUSE...

After some time,
One would think,
That cloud WOULDN'T still be,
Right IN THAT very SAME spot!,

THAT(BY NOW!)...(It SHOULD HAVE)...(drifted along!)...

'CAUSE...

((That WAS his VERY NEXT thought!!))

And(At the VERY LEAST!)...

It WOULDN'T (STILL!) look,
EXACTLY the same!!,
Continuing to sit there,
Looking up into that gigantic cloud,
Becoming more and more amazed!!,

That...
He IS looking INTO a gigantic face!

And...

It kinda' freaks him out (a bit),

Thinking, to himself,...

"THERE'S, a face IN that cloud!,
Yes! This IS real!",...

And...

He KNOWS as though,
AS HE IS watching,
HE IS being watched,
(THAT'S just HOW he feels!!),

(And these are his thoughts!)(OF: His vision!)(As he began to write!)...
(COME!)...Let's go inside his mind:

And, it's a beautiful day. Bright blue beautiful sky! Kinda' chilly. Kinda' breezy. Which makes the stratus clouds, TRAVEL SLOWLY, from left to right, in the sky. (BUT, not this cloud!). THIS is a cumulus cloud! (The one that, kinda' looks like, it DEFINITELY has two eyes!)...(A nose!!)...(A mouth!!!)...(AND, a jaw-line!!!!) And, I ain't never seen a cloud that big, AND BE SO LOW, to the ground!!!!!

And, of this, I AM sure, as I first sat there, that giant cloud, WASN'T there before! And, as it's presence was felt, I felt as though, I WASN'T sitting there by myself. And, as I looked up, all of the other clouds, WERE gently traveling-on, from left to right. (BUT, NOT THIS CLOUD!!!) For, THIS cloud, STAYED in that very same spot! (And, besides that, IT WAS all by itself!) And, no other cloud, traveled in front of it. (Of that face, no other cloud, obscured my vision and sight) As, all of the stratus clouds, (on THAT morning!) traveled-on, FROM left to right! And, as I sat there, I became deep in thought. And, I thought of what to write. After I kept looking up at that cloud, this is what, my deep thought brought: The cloud was either the Virgin Mary, Jesus or my Dad. (But, by Dad, perhaps, I was actually thinking, Father God).

And so...

Turning the page,
In his black and white composition book,
He continued to write:

FOR, WHEN

I was born a shy and withdrawn kid,
Had no idea of the things,
The world would have did,
Kept a carved-up Bible and a BIG knife hid,
(You think THAT'S harsh???),
(((THIS world is VICIOUS!!!))),

SO...

I learned THAT the world,
Was FULL of strife,...

AND...

YOU GOT-DAMN-RIGHT,
I became THE MOST mutha' fuckin' trife!!!,

BUT...

Hangin' ONTO bitterness,
IS a waste of life!,

(I KNOW Y'ALL WANT to live this!)...

BUT...

((Y'all BETTER think twice!!))...

AIN'T no shame,
IN MY mutha' fuckin' game!,
Live with regret?,
OR keep it FUCKIN' pushin'?,
(IT'S ALL the same!),
YOU learn, if YOU live,

So...

(I'MA break it down simple and plain)...

The world's GONNA' know me,
Just as long as GOD KNOWS my name!,

IF YOU EVER want to know what Heaven looks like?,
Just look up at the morning sky,
And look up at the bright son light,
And look up at that bright blue screen of blue,
And look up at those big white clouds of fluffy,

And I have no fear,
For, when I meet God,
There will be no lie in me,
No lie in me,
No lie in me,
I HAVE NO fear of thee,
For, when I meet God,
There will be no lie in me,
No lie in me,
No lie in me,
I have NO fear of thee,
For, when I meet God,
There will be no lie in me,

(My Mom died on a Sunday,
Her, "Great getting up morning",
"Rod, I won't be 'round forever.",
"Mom, thanks for the warning.",
She said, "I won't be around forever.",
I said, "Mom, thanks for the warning.")...

And so...

I look up at the sky EVERY morning,
'Cause I KNOW He checks on me,
'Cause THROUGH those fluffy clouds,
I KNOW He takes a peek,
And when I see big fluffy clouds,
I KNOW THAT'S Heaven coming through!,
And I look for the son shining down,
Against a screen of morning blue,
AND when I look at the morning son,
I KNOW what I HAVE TO DO,
I say, "Good morning, Jesus!",

For...

The morning son has returned to see,
IF OUR Faith IS true!,

WHO to trust?,
Who TO trust??,
Who to TRUST???,

NEVER rush!,
Never RUSH!!,
NEVER RUSH!!!,

IF IT looks like what it is,
THEN it is,
If it SOUNDS LIKE what it is,
You're BEING disrespected!,

And so...

For that,
IF I don't HAVE,
YOU GO ON,

AND KEEP,
YOUR "illusion" OF love!,

For...

I KNOW,
In who,
I TRUST!,

"Good morning, Jesus!", said,
EVERY MORNING,
To THE Son!,

And...

(IF YOU'RE FAKE-AS-FUCK??)...

KEEP YOUR OLIVE BRANCH,
AND YOUR FUCKIN' PEACE DOVE!!,

AND...

YES, I AM A SOLDIER OF,
THE ONE UP ABOVE!!,

BUT...

DIG IT,
WHEN IT COMES TO REAL SHIT?,
YES, I AM A WITNESS,

BUT...

(DON'T GIVE A FUCK ABOUT NO WITNESSES;)

So...

I don't GIVE A FUCK 'bout your rejections!,

For...

NOW I'M callin' tha' shots,
AND I'M MAKIN' tha' selections!,

And so...

(I'MA break it down, simple and plain!)...

THE world's gonna know me,
Just as long as GOD KNOWS my name!,

IF YOU EVER want to know what Heaven looks like?,
Just look up at the morning sky,
And look up at the bright son light,
And look up at that screen of blue,
And at the big white clouds of fluffy,
AND I have NO fear!,
For, when I meet God,
There WILL BE no lie in me,
NO lie in me,
NO lie in me,
I have NO fear of THEE,
For, when I meet God,
There WILL BE no lie in me,
NO lie in me,
NO lie in me,
I HAVE NO FEAR OF THEE!!!!!!,
For, when I meet God,
There WILL BE no lie in me.

And(On that note!)...
(*YOU HAVE JUST READ the world's MOST FUCKED-UP gospel!*)...

Though...

(A gospel, ALL the same!)

THERE'S A SWARM ON ITS WAY

FOR...

THERE AIN'T SHIT,
THAT you CAN give,
OR offer,
OR provide,
TO GET THESE FOUR TO ABIDE!!!!,

For...

(They ARE in, and, of themselves!!!!)

AND...

(They make life ON earth a LIVING hell!!!!)

FOR...

AT THIS VERY SECOND THEY RIDE!!!!,
Two columns AT two abreast,
With one hand on a steel HORSE throttle OPEN WIDE!!!!,
With the other hand MIDDLE FINGER IN THE AIR!!!!,
WITH THE WIND beaten-off OF their,
WHITE, BRIGHT RED, BLACK, and PALE,
Vintage Prohibition Era-style gangster suits,
And beaten-off OF their suspenders,
And beaten-off OF their three-piece vests!!!!,
And they're traveling at BREAKNECK-BLINDING-SPEED!!!!,
WITH THE FOUR,
TO TROTTLES WIDE-OPEN HANGIN' ON!!!!,
WITH THE FOUR, STRAIGHT-UP-LIFTING-UP -
CLEAR OUT OF THEIR SEATS!!!!,

AND...

((((DO NOT GET IT TWISTED))))...

FOR...

((((THERE IS, AND, CAN BE ONLY ONE,
TO THAT, AND OF, THEY LISTEN!!!!))))

AND...

THAT IS, AND, THE ONLY WAY, IT IS!!!!

FOR....

THEY ARE HERE, AND, THEY ARE REAL!!!!

AND...

((((OF THEM, THERE IS NO PRETEND!!!!))))....

AND....

IT IS THE FOUR'S MISSION,

TO MAKE YOU PRAY,
THAT "YOU" WERE NEVER BORN!!!!,

AND....

((((OF THIS, I DO NOT KID!!!!))))

FOR...

There's A swarm ON ITS way!!!!,
OF flying BUZZING bugs!!!!,
((((HOW MANY, YOU ask????)))),
ENOUGH TO blockout the sun!!!!,

FOR(YOU SEE!!!!)...

THERE'S A storm,...

AND DISEASE,...
AND a skelton CLUTCHIN' his rib bones,
GETTIN'-BEATEN-UP BY THE WIND,
((((TO AND FROW!!!!)))), BEING THROWN,
FROM AND OF, THE BLACK FLAG,
GETTIN' SHREADED-DOWN TO A RAG,
ON THE BACK OF CHOPPER,
THE COLOR IS BLACK!!!!,
FROM POPPED-CLUTCHES,
AND FROM THROTTLES WIDE-OPEN!!!!,
Leaving YOU WITH dispare,
WITH NO hope,...
AND YET hoping!!!!!!!,
WITH,...FEELINGS OF anger!!!!,
(Gonna-gotcha' QUESTIONING YOUR FAITH!!!!),....

AS((((TO WHY????))))....

YOU LOST,
WHAT YOU LOST,
AND ((((WHY????)))) IN YOUR MIND,
YOU WERE ALLOWED TO BE SO WRONGED????,
AND, FOR AND OF,
IF you did and,
IF you EVEN thought of,
((((HOW COME it ain't????)))),
And, WHATEVER MADE YOU BELIEVE that,...
YOUR FAITH was EVER STRONG????,

For(You See)...

They are gangsters from the old school,
The one in **WHITE** is out to **CONQUER**,
(And he can do it!),

'Cause he's already conquered "Cool" and "Smooth"!!!!,

The one in **BRIGHT RED**,
WANTS TO wage **WAR** and see YOU dead!!!!,
And he don't give a fuck what YOU want,
He's out to wage WAR in a rage,
And it's for YOU he's on the hunt!!!!,

The one in all **BLACK**,
Got a sick sense of humor,
He'd rather **STARVE** and thurst YOU!!!!,
Before he gives you a drink or snack,
Which he won't!,
(Told y'all he gets off on sick jokes!),
He wants to see your ribs embossed in your skin,
And with your lips with deep long painful cracks!!!!,

And then you got the one that rocks all **PALE**,
And he's the type TO **BURY** ALL OF YOU!!!!,
In the hot-ass desert,
WITH a shovel and pale,
In tiny brass urns,
For YOU to FOREVER burn!!!!,

((((OH, YES!!!!))))....((((HAVE fear, my dear!!!!))))

FOR,...

((((They WERE put here!!!!))))....((((TO CAUSE FEAR!!!!))))

((((AND THEY'RE ON THEIR WAY!!!!))))....((((THE END IS NEAR!!!!))))

FOR(YOU SEE!!!!)....

THESE FOUR RIDERS,
HAVE BEEN SUMMOMENED,
TO TAKE whatever AND TO WITHOLD,
whatever THEY WANT,
((((FROM YOU!!!!)))),

FOR....

THEY DO WHAT THEY WANT TO DO!!!!

AND....

PLEASE, YOU BEST-BELIEVE, that,....
THEY'LL DO IT TO YOU!!!!

EARTH, WIND, AND FIRE *(THE DECEIVER)*

The power of power,
The devil was made for moments like these,
And at the necessary moments in time,
The devil applies that power,
Having the power to deceive,...

You, yes YOU,
YOU can leave if you want,
But listen to me,
Why don't you have seat back down,
On that fine red leather love seat,

I'll pop some champagne,
(You know what I'm sayin;)
OR I have some vintage wine,
(If YOU'D prefer!),
Yes! SIT!!! 'Cause THIS time,...
I want YOU to sit down next to her!,

Us three will just sit and talk,
And to persude you not to walk,
We'll take our time, on some fine cigars,
I want you to get to know who we are,
And I'll put on some relaxing tunes,
To set the mood in this all-red-everythang room!,...

AS...

The man in custom red,
Puts on some Earth, Wind and, Fire,
Explaining, as he, says,...
"It's a name,...that conjures,...and inspires.",...

"That name, in tongues, it talks to me,
Ain't no, faux pas,
It just has a certain, Je ne sais pas,
Wouldn't you agree?",...

"You have the earth.,
You have the wind.,
And then you have the fire.",...

"Which one is more important than the other?,
Can one exist without the other?,
The fire needs the wind to feed it,
Wouldn't you agree?",...

"For you see,
The fire can't grow and build and rage,
Without the food,
Of the wind,
Provided over the ages.",...

"That fire,
That fire,
In the pit of hell",...

"That fire,
That fire,
Is the earth's heart itself!",...

"That fire,
That fire,
Comes out of the earth",...

To "check" the earth!,
It POURS over the earth!!,
It runs OVER the earth!!!,

And powerless against the fire,...
IS the earth!",...

"That fire,
That fire,
Puts the earth on notice.",...

"And the earth,
Can't do a damn thing about it!",
("In the event,
You've never noticed;)

"The four winds of the earth,
Where would they be?,
If for not for the earth,
Across to sweep,
To bend every blade of grass,
And to pass through all the leaves.",...

"For you see,
It's the earth,
That gives the four winds purpose.,
If not for the earth,
Where would the four winds blow?",...

"Lost. Rutterless. And aimless.
Where would the four winds go?,
Up in outer space,
Some place,
I suppose.",...

"Since the birth,
Of the earth,
It's the earth,
Providing the four winds,

With a sense of being.",...

"But you must see,
Without the four winds,
The earth wouldn't be.,
Wouldn't you agree?",...

"And then you have,
The earth itself.,
And it's THAT fire,
Burning and churning,
Down in the pit of itself!",...

"For you see,
The heart of the earth,
Is the fire",...

"In dire need,
Of the wind,
For to feed.",...

"The wind needs the earth,
To give it direction,
To guide the wind where to go,
For its own protection.",...

"For you see,
I'm really not so bad of a man.",
(Says the man in custom red),...
"With direction and guidance,
I'm just trying to provide YOU,
I hope YOU understand.",...

"YOU ARE the wind!,
Why ARE YOU holding yourself back,

FROM blowing all over the earth???",...

"BE the wind!,
Kick-up some dust AND some static!!,
Worse than a curse,...
Is choosing TO BE stagnant!!!",...

"Blow over the earth!,
MAKE IT spin!,
YOU AND I are in this together!!,
YOU ARE the wind!",...

"I AM the fire!,
And together WE SHALL cover the earth!!,
You'll have all that YOU desire,...
But I'ma need your soul first."

NOTHING LIKE YOU

You look upon me with eyes of scorn.
I'm me.
That's ALL I'm trying to be.

Sooooooo...

I don't know,
What YOUR looks OF scorn,
ARE for!?!,

You judge me!,
WHEN YOU shall not!!,
YOU'RE NOT THE ONE approved to DO so!!!,

(((LET the sinking begin - OF - that thought!)))...

Against ME,
YOU cast stones upon!,
In doing so,...
Me OR you??,
WHO'S in the wrong??,

FOR...

One with two ears and,
With a too-eagar-to-hear-hearsay-brain,
ONE IS DOOMED TO do AS sheeps AND robots DO,
All the same!!,

And so...

(Upon the sheep and robo I do so bestow)...

For...

IF YOU'RE ONE that falls in THAT category,
ONE to believe and do,
Based on what you hear,...

Well...

(((Let me make THIS very clear!!!)))...

My fists ARE clinched!!

As...

I too, hold the rocks,

'Cause...

I too, CAN CAST STONES UPON!!!

Now...

(((LET the sinking begin - OF - THAT thought!)))...

AND SO...

Should I, cast stones,
As, YOU do?,
Should I, judge,
WHEN, I shall not!!!,
TO judge???,
AS, YOU do!!!,

BUT...

My head, looks North,

As...

I, pray on it,...

My rocks fall South,

FROM…

MY clinched fists!!,

As…

I, release my grip,

Because…

I KNOW,
There's ONLY ONE,
TO judge!,

(THIS, I know, IS true!!!)

So…

I cast. NO stones.

And(IT'S because)…

…I don't want to be like you.
Amen.

SPOILS

I work hard for these spoils,
Even if it means in the Lake of Fire I'ma boil,
Even down in that bitch I'm toil,
Catch me down in that bitch on my toil,
Have the devil comin' back,
'Cause I keep 'em loyal,
Have that mother fucker kissin' my pinky ring,
'Cause I'm Royal,
Have the devil kissin' my fuckin' pinky ring,
'CAUSE I'M ROYAL!!!

LEARN

I am the nails and the cross,
The pain and blood loss,
The head raked with thorns,
The hatered, the scorn,

I'm the Sloth and Envy,
I'm the Wrath best believe,
I'm a Glutton for Lust,
I am the full-fledged Greed,

Was that Six of the Seven?,
Oh yeah, I'm the Pride,
I'm the holes in the feet,
I'm the spear in the side,

And if God wants me,
To go to hell and burn?,
Then that's where I'll go,
'Cause that's where I'll learn,...

Of how much,
God really loved me,
Because this is what,
He wanted for me,

Of all the people,
God thought of me,
And this is where,
He wanted me to be,

So this is where I'll stay,
And this is where I'll burn,
Because God thought enough of me,
To send me here to learn.

PUNISHED

Meanwhile in Hell…

He lies there on his back,
Breathing in,
The sulfur suffocating depths of it all,

From his millenniums in Hell,
The embers of his charred body,
Have formed in shape,
And have hardened in place,
Into an empty shell,
Of his former earthly self,
Now and for all eternity,
Made of brimstone.
Punished.

His eyes are the only physical tissue he has left,
Of his earthly human form,
His bones, blood, muscle, hair and flesh,
And lastly his organs,
Have long since slowly burned away,
From his time in Hell through the ages.
Punished.

His earthly eyes,
Smoldered into and fixed in place,
Inside of his brimstone eye sockets,
Have retained the gift of sight.
Punished.

Damned and taught,
With sight and thought,

And that of his hearing,
And that of pain,
Of an entire nervous system set on fire,
For all of eternity,
Over and over again,
He lies there,
Fully conscious and aware,
Stacked in the pit of Hell,
As tiny fire demons dance across,
Hell's dance floor,
Dancing like a groom with no bride,
Crackling as they cackle,
While they lance him,
With their tiny pitchforks of fire.
Punished.

These tiny hate-filled demons never cease,
Stabbing his brimstone face and chest,
With tiny pitchforks made of fire,
Enjoying themselves to say the least,
They laugh wildly,
They never stop their torment,
His eyes fixed in place force him,
To forever stare directly towards,
The upper shelf of Hell,
Through his brimstone eye sockets,
Of his for all eternity brimstone self.
Punished.

His brimstone body,
Bears the weight of his sins,
And, that too,
Of the myriads and myriads of souls,

Encased in the hollowed-out-brimstone-bodied shells,
Of such sinners,
Such as himself,
Condemned to Hell,
And, to wit,
Comprise the floor of Hell's pit,
Along with he.
Punished.

These brimstone bodies,
Parched, encrusted, not rotting,
Burning in Hell,
At the very bottom,
All gnarled, stacked,
Fused-together-shells,
Comprise of and makeup,
The floor of Hell.
Punished.

For...

Satan awaits them,...

FOR...

(((GOD HAS PREPARED A PLACE FOR THEM!!!)))

And...

It's called the Floor of Hell!,...

FOR...

(((SINNERS SUCH AS YOURSELF!!!)))

AND SO...

The brimstone floor of Hell,
Continues to slowly grow,
Like the Great Barrier Reef,
Seemingly impossible,
But, yet possible,
Because it's forever growing,
Forever tortured,
At no time is his sight obscured,
As a result,
Of this continued growth,
Over the ages.
Punished.

Through the smoke and fire demons,
At the edge of the black and burgundy of Hell,
Is the light of Heaven,...

Through the demons,
Through the stacked-shelled-souls of the damned,
Through the suffocating burning smoke of sulfur,
Through this millennia,
And through the millenniums,
Beyond those millenniums,
And through the millenniums,
Beyond those millenniums ahead,
And beyond those milleniums,
And through and beyond those millenniums still,
He's forced to stare up towards Heaven,
By his earthly eyes,
Encased inside,
Of brimstone eye sockets,
At a gigantic,
Evergreen tree standing there,

Straight ahead.
Punished.

In and within his eternal view,
Massively placed,
Directly above the gigantic evergreen tree,
Is the gigantic head of God,
Clear within his eternal sight,
Formed from clouds,
And beaming golden light,

God's mouth slams open and shut,
As His words rumble as thunder,
Rumbling within,
His charred and embered-sinned -
Brimstoned-bodied soul-damned - shell,
Of his former earthly self,

Each time,
The mouth of God opens and slams shut,
Lightning bolts of the likes never seen,
Shoot from the mouth of God like laser beams,
Striking the brimstone floor,
In the pit depths of Hell,
Creating more fire demons,
In which,
To torment,
The hollowed-out-damned-souled-brimstoned-shells,
Of the sinner's former earthly-selves,
And, does so,
By increasing depth,
To the lake of fire's depth,
In the pit depths of Hell.

Punished.

For...

Satan awaits them,...

FOR...

(((GOD HAS PREPARED A PLACE FOR THEM!!!)))

And...

It's called the Floor of Hell!,...

FOR...

(((SINNERS SUCH AS YOURSELVES!!!)))

AND SO...

Through this millennia,
And through the millenniums,
Beyond those millenniums,
And beyond and through,
Those millenniums still ahead,
And beyond and through those millenniums,
And beyond and through those millenniums beyond,
He is forced to stare up at,
The gigantic evergreen tree that,
In Heaven grows,
As an eternal reminder for him to know,
That he had lived a life of sin.
Punished.

For...

The winter trees,
In the dead of winter,

All lose their leaves,
And appear as though dead,

Though...

(NOT the evergreen tree!)...

FOR...

The evergreen tree,
In the dead of winter,
Does not appear as though alive,

For...

The evergreen tree,
Remains forever green,
Fully and provides,
What is needed to survive,

For...

The evergreen tree,
Remains forever green,
When all that is green,
In the dead of winter,
Appears as though it has died,

And so...

The gigantic head of God,
Formed by clouds and beaming golden light,
Shouts directly at his brimstone body,
Forged into the floor of Hell,
The gigantic hinged-jaw of God slams open and shut,
Over and over again,
Making the sound of thunder every time it slams shut,

Every time God opens His mouth,
The deafening words of God blasts and rings,
Inside of his brimstone head,
God's rapid fire words,
Are never ending,
Lightning strikes shoot out,
Of God's mouth,
Creating more fire in Hell,
God's words are deafening,
Like firecrackers set off in a coffee can,
Over and over again,
God shouts at his brimstone body demanding,
That he listen to God's words and commanding,
That he continually,
Look only at this gigantic evergreen tree,
That his eyes shall forever be fixed on,
For ALL ETERNITY,
God tells his brimstone body,
That the evergreen tree is to remind him,
That if he had only followed the word of God,
Then, he too,
Would have had everlasting life in Heaven,...

And so...

Through and beyond this millennia,
And through and beyond the millenniums,
Still ahead of those millenniums still ahead,
And through and beyond,
Those millenniums ahead of those millenniums,
And through and beyond those millenniums,
Beyond and through those millenniums still ahead,...

(((HE GETS TO LIE THERE LIKE THAT!!!)))

WITH thought, hearing, pain and sight,
With earthy eyes,
Melted, molded and fixed in place,
Of the brimstone eye sockets,
Of his soul-damned-shelled-brimstone body,
(and look and learn),
As the evergreen tree lives on,
Forever green,
Providing what is needed to survive,
And know that due to,
The life of sin he's lived,
That he wasn't provided,
With everlasting life.
Punished.

For...

Trees lose their leaves,
In the dead of winter,
And appear as though dead,...

BUT...

(NOT the evergreen tree!)...

For...

The evergreen tree,
Forever remains,
Forever green,...

Punished by sight, sound, pain and thought,
He lies on his back in the depths of Hell.
Punished.

DUST OFF THE BIBLE

Should I knock the dust off the Bible?,
'Cause its been awhile,
Sitting here thinking about,
My tribulations and trials,
And the pain I'm in,
Went insane again,
Bathe me in your blood Lord,
And wash away my sin,

Drugs, bullets, booze,
I put them all in me,
Just to wake up the next day,
What a travesty,
Death wish my entire life,
But it keeps evading me,
When you're ready Lord,
I'm ready Lord,
Take me home with Thee,

Misled, used and hurt,
By you people on earth,
I want to kill you all,
But that's too much work,
The first shall be last,
And the last shall be first,
And on the day I finally die,
Will be the date of my birth,

And don't blame me,
For my mental disease,
For my bipolar,

And my split personalities,
I'll end up burning in Hell,
While praying on my knees,
At the right hand of the devil,
While begging Jesus please,
If I make it to hell,
Heaven will freeze,
Think what you want,
But only God can judge me,

I'll go out fully engulfed,
And like that Monk,
I won't move or wail,
I'll make it to Heaven,
After purgatory's jail,
Arms stretched out,
Looking up at,
100 pound stone hail,
Won't even give a fuck,
'Cause I've lived this tale,

Who's real anymore,
With all this fake-a-rie?,
All you sheeps and robots,
Are a disgrace to me,
On my tombstone,
Let it read: 1967 - FREE,
And for the ones,
That really cared,
Thank you for praying for me.

THOUGHTS

IT AIN'T

It is,
What,
It is,

No.
It ain't.

You think,
That,
It is,

But,
I'm telling you,
It ain't.

Don't believe,
Everything,
You hear,

After all,
The Titanic,
Sank,

You think,
That,
It is,

But,
I'm telling you,
It ain't.

Too many,
Sheeps and robots,
Walkin' 'round,
With their minds,
Blank,...

Don't sail blind,
Into darkness,
That's how,
The Titanic,
Sank,...

It is,
What,
It is,

No.
It ain't.

You think,
That,
It is,

But,
I'm telling you,
It ain't.

FUCK Y'ALL

"Many that selfishly,
Live for today,
Ruin a many,
Of many's tomorrows." - RHW

THE HUSTLE

"The music game and the drug game,
Are one in the same.
Where you find music,
You find drugs.
And it's all just one big hustle." - RHW

CARE TAKEN

"Caretakers" taking care, alright!
TAKING CARE of some shopping!
WHILE the ones THAT can stand care,
And NOT alright - IN NEED of care,
Stand neglected - Taken to the mall,
WHILE the state gets taken!

A COMEDY OF ERRS

"Everybody's funny,
when it comes to money.
And the bigger the money,
the funnier they are." - RHW

"All-The-Timey"

""Sometimey" people,
Are ALWAYS "sometimey".
But sometimes,
They remind you,
Of how "sometimey" they really are." - RHW

W@R

"I'm at war against ignorance." - RHW

"CASUALLY OF WAR"

Gotta avoid bullet holes,
Gotta avoid running -
Outta camera rolls,
(Gotta go digital!),
Gotta avoid those bombs,
Thee creators -
Of all of those -
Craterous holes!,

All While(And ALL THE WHILE)...

Gotta avoid capture,
Gotta avoid my soul,
Being lifted -
Clear-up -
To the sky -
Like the rapture!,
(And yet - capture!),

For(You See)...

Once I find the right,
Moment in-frame,
(IF I get lucky!),
I'll have the time -
To do more than just to -
"Raise n' Aim"!,

For(YOU See!)...

To capture the day -
Thru the night -

TO STAY alive -
Is a brave soul's job -
We're brave souls,
Avoiding bullet holes,
SO MUCH MORE -
THAN "Raise n' Aim"!,
            So much more than a job,
                (And you find THAT out right-quick -
            ONCE the grenades are lobbed!),

For(YOU SEE)...

From the sea -
To the inner city -
From the deserts -
To the outskirts -
Brave souls,
Are down in the thick of it all,
Down in the Aires that are Buenos -
All the way up to the Himalayas!, -

Brave souls,
Are more than adventurers,
But don't call us courageous,
(YOU CAN'T contain us!),
THIS path IS contagious!,
With a photographic eye,
That's the way God made us!,

For(You See)...

If it's heinous?,
There ain't NO hiatus!,
Can you blame us??,

MOST brave souls are nameless!,

AND SO...

Brave souls,
WE GO!!!,
To the massacre in Vegas,
(Gotta make the shutter click!),
Once got a tip on a precinct,
That: THAT'S WHERE the flames is!,

SO...

(Please don't place shame on us shamus!)

FOR(YOU SEE!!)...

Brave souls,
GOTTA GO!!!,
Capture the pics the most-efficacious,
That'll make us the most-famous!!!,

And so(AND BUT NOW!)...

There's a citywide blackout,...

Soooooo...

(My camera's flash is NOT allowed!)

AND...

Supposedly the fires were supposed to cease?,...

Soooooo...

(WHY are those explosions STILL loud!?!)

For(You See)...

Based on that -
(Due to thee NO-LET-UP of that!),...
We were all forced to flee -
To the basements of these -
"Shelled-Out" apartments -
Due to all thee bombardments!,

And(ALTHOUGH!)...

I'm not TRYING TO get wasted,...
MY time IS BEING wasted!,
MADE TO hunker down -
(AND - Shelter-in-place!),
IN - AND - OF - THIS -
Bunker-Make-Shift-Basement!,

For(You See)...

(Not-so-much for me)...

BUT...

(I've got to get back out to "the shit"!)...

'Cause...

((LEST WE FORGET!!))...

Certain factions,
On freedom of speech,
In certain places,
Severe infractions,
Have been placed!,

AND SO...

(Of and for those of whom to are being lied?)...

Well...

(((I'VE GOT TO GO GIVE THIS FISHEYE LENS A TRY!!!)))

And so...

OK...(I Know)...(I'LL KNOW right where to go!)...

Just gotta ride out the night,...

For...

(When the lighting is right!)

And...

I won't need no maps nor schematics!!,...

For(YOU SEE!!)...

I'LL JUST follow that trail of black smoke,...

FROM...

(((THE BOMBINGS over a few days ago!!!)))

For(((You See!!!)))...

(In a city park)...(in the next city)...(over)...(parked in the center of the city!),...

I saw some swings,...

(((That have been maimed!!!)))

Along with a jungle gym,...

(((That'll never look the same!!!)))

THOUGH...

(It WON'T be from!)

Its new paint job,
Spray painted AND stained,
FROM ALL the blood,
AND the brain!!,

AND...

(It WON'T be from!)

The occupants' rockets that dropped,
In thee exact same spot! -
Occupied once by children -
And all the other civilians -
(That are no longer living:(

MADE TO shift a maternity ward,
Into a bomb shelter,
Huddled together,
Woman and child,
Hungry and horrified,
By those rockets in the night sky!,

WHICH...

MAKES the shape of the huddle shift!,
Underground down on the floor,
MADE TO MAKE a make-shift -
Materinty-Bomb-Shelter-Ward!,

Women with child,
Won't see their babies born,
'Cause all of them died,
Yup - ALL THOSE CIVILIANS - (Aren't living no more:(

And...

(Oh, Sure!)

Symbolically assembled sunflower billboards are nice!,

And...

(Oh, Sure!)

Buildings locally - Bridges globally -
Monuments - Lit up - Symbolically -
WITH - Blue and Yellow lights -
Sure do look nice!,

Buuuuuut...

((That has about AS MUCH "effictiveness-in-semblance"))...

AS...

A bowl of rice - held-in-hand - by the Distended-Stomach-Kid -
WITH - fly larvae in his eyes!!,

AS...

The: Hungry - The: Don't-Have-Money -
The: Unsure - The: Alone - AND - The: War-Torn-Poor -
WITH - Higher expectations - FROM - The West -
For another night of fighting - DO SO - PREP!,...

As...

They prep for fire from up above THEIR town,...
UPON THEM ONCE MORE to shower down!,

As...

Everything from their kitchens - (INCLUDING the kitchen sink!),
FROM LAST NIGHT'S fighting - HAVE BEEN blownout into the street!,

As...

(((IT'S JUST AS WELL!!!)))

AS...

THESE: Don't-Have-Money-War-Torn-Poor - ARE - SO poor,...
THEY: (((HAVEN'T HAD NO FOOD TO PREP TO EAT!!!))),

AS...

The "Powers That Be" - AND - The "Pullers-of-the-Strings",...
Stay spending the tax payers' money - Prepping FOR WAR steadily!,

AS...

ALL of THAT preparation,...
HAS TURNED into THEIR manifestation!,

AS...

The "Powers That Be" - AND - The "Pullers-of-the-Strings",...
Eat up MORALS! POWER!! MONEY!!! AND GREED!!!!,

AS...

The poor are forced to see - The bursting of gluttony's seams,...
In the form of bursting bombs - By that well-fed fucking WAR MACHINE!!!,

As...

This city's at its limit!,

As...

This will be now the second time - In history -
The Russians have now breached - This city's limits!,

AS...

((THIS WILL BE NOW - FOR - THE SECOND TIME!!))

THAT...

THIS city: WILL HAVE BEEN in ruins -
BY: ((The hands - OF - the Russian's doings!!)),

((Oy vey!!))

As...

Communications ARE in disarray!,...

As...

(((The Russian's stalled-out truck convoys AREN'T a good "Global look"!!!)))

(Yeah)...(so)...(uh)...(well)...(NOW)...(anywaaaaaays),...

(((THAT'S ABOUT WHAT all the Mass-Media-Airwaves HAVE TO say!!!)))

As...

Nobody NOW knows who's running the Russian's headquarters!?!,

As...

There's MANY MORE Russian Troops stagged JUST OVER the borders!,

As...

In-country there are many major Russian Troops present!,

As...

The Ukraine residents - ARE FORCE FED WITH FORCE - the Russian's SHIT!!,

As...

((Butt cheeks GET clinched!!))...

AS...

((Butt holes ARE cinched!!))...

Juxtapose...

(To the major Russian Troops TANK CONVOY MOVEMENTS of many of those!)

Juxtapose...

The Ukraine residents - FEEL THE RUMBLINGS - of a presence,...

Apropos...

AS((IF))...

((They're ABOUT TO HAVE - A MAJOR MOVEMENT - of their own!!)) -

((Oy vey!!))

AS...

The bowels of the people have become impacted with traffic!,

AS...

The movements of the Ukrainian-Refugee-Crisis-Exodus continues in mass!,

AS...

Families are forced to flee from their own homeland and cities!,

BUT...

((NOT IF YOUR - MALE - FAMILY - MEMBERS - RANGE IN AGES - 18 - 60!!))

AS...

(((THE - HUGS - KISSES - CRIES - AND - GOODBYE'S - HAVE - STATRED!!!)))

AS...

(((THE - FAMILIES - OF - THE - UKRAINE - ARE - BEING - TORN - APART!!)))

As(FOR)...

(Those ABLE to flee?)...((One of the LAST THINGS they'll see!!)),...

As(FOR)...

(((SURELY TO FOREVER BE!!!))) - ((((IN ALL their memories!!!!)))),...

AS...

They travel past,...

AS...

(By on foot or by other means of transit),...

AS...

((From THEIR Homeland - AND - Cities they go!!)),...

WILL BE the pleasant sight - OF - Refrigerated tractor trailers - Parked together - In a long line - Along the sides of THEIR roads,...

THEREIN...

Contents containing - (((FROM OFF THE SIDES OF THEIR ROADS!!!))) -
The contents of those - Collected in-part,...
OF - (((THE MANY RUSSIAN SOLDIERS TORN APART!!!))),

(((OY VEY!!!)))

And...(YET!)...

There's just something 'bout those swings,
(That STILL resonates with me!),...

And...

That too of the jungle gym -
(Of it to it to of it - it was next!),...

AS...

((They were both made - TO - never look the same!!))

From all those hypersonic missiles -
Shot from all those hypersonic planes!!,

ALTHOUGH((AND SO!!))...

(It WON'T be from!!)

Them both being all twisted and gnarled!!,

For(YOU See!)...

It's the tank tracks in the ground,
That crisscross the playground,
That bears "the fruits of the (war) crimes" - it's immoral!,

And...(APPARENTLY!)...

Nurses...(((ARE SCARY!!!)))

(TO the Generals IN general!),...

(((ALONG WITH the school kids!!!)))

'CAUSE...

(((WHAT I've found through MY viewfinder!!!))),...

(In-frame of thee invading occupiers!),...

OF those occupants -
OF the nurses -
OF the school kids -

Well...

(((THAT'S WHERE THEIR AIM IS!!!)))

'CAUSE...

A few days back,...
OF WHICH - TO WHICH,
(Once the light is right!),...
I'm gonna double back!!,

For((YOU SEE!!))...

I've captured some pics,
Of a Mass-Grave-Trench,...

For...

Over all those dead school kids,...
(WERE the sounds MADE BY)...(my shutter's clicks!),...

Albeit...

(Over THEM)...(COVERING them)...(WERE OTHER dead civilians:(

Albeit...

(By the dead BEING)...

Lowered-down and covered-up -

Up on the lip of the trench -
BY all the other civilians -
(AFTER the latest fighting round!) -
LUCKY ENOUGH TO HAVE FOUND -
Themselves TO STILL be living!!!, -

Albeit...

The covered -
Whom were covered -
WERE covered -
(By body bags and shoveled dirt:(

AND...

To the best that I could see,...
(((I BELIEVE!!!))) -
(EACH of the remaining body bags -
EACH one contained a nurse:(

AND SO...

Gotta avoid bullet holes,
Gotta avoid running -
Outta camera rolls,
(Gotta go digital!),
Gotta avoid those bombs,
Thee creators -
Of all of those -
Craterous holes!,

All While(And ALL THE WHILE)...

Gotta avoid capture,
Gotta avoid my soul,
Being lifted -

Clear-up -
To the sky -
Like the rapture!,
(And yet - capture!),

For(You See)...

Once I find the right,
Moment in-frame,
(IF I get lucky!),
I'll have the time -
To do more than just to -
"Raise n' Aim"!,

For(YOU See!)...

To capture the day -
Thru the night -
TO STAY alive -
Is a brave soul's job -
We're brave souls,
Avoiding bullet holes,
SO MUCH MORE -
THAN "Raise n' Aim"!,

So much more than a job,
(And you find THAT out right-quick -
ONCE the Molotov cocktails are lobbed!),

For(YOU SEE)...

From the sea -
To the inner city -
From the deserts -
To the outskirts -
Brave souls,

Are down in the thick of it all,
Down in the Aires that are Buenos -
All the way up to the Himalayas!, -

Brave souls,
Are more than adventurers,
But don't call us courageous,
(YOU CAN'T contain us!),
THIS path IS contagious!,
With a photographic eye,
That's the way God made us!,

For(You See)...

If it's heinous?,
There ain't NO hiatus!,
Can you blame us??,
MOST brave souls are nameless!,

AND SO...

Brave souls,
WE GO!!!,
To the massacre in Vegas,
(Gotta make the shutter click!),
Once got a tip on a precinct,
That: THAT'S WHERE the flames is!,

SO...

(Please don't place shame on us shamus!)

FOR(YOU SEE!!)...

Brave souls,
GOTTA GO!!!,

Capture the pics the most-efficacious,
That'll make us the most-famous!!!,

And so...(And)...((I'LL BE DAMNED!!))...

OF ALL the warnings -
Of suppressions -
To the Russians -
Have done nothing -
To Suppress -
ALL OF the air raid warnings!,

And...

(As of)...

Yesterday morning,...

(As for)...

What Putin's STILL BEEN banking on,...

Well...

(As FOR it!)...((IS FOR!!))...(((NATO TO BE SPLIT!!!))),

AS...

The banks of the Kremlin -
And the "Oligarchs of Privilege"! -
(The Russian's version -
OF: The "Pullers of the Strings"!) -
ARE being - getting - AND - GOT stripped!,
Shiiiiiit! - (((Drones MAY have been lofted AND sent!!!))) -
TO GO collect the rent - OF - "THEE loftiest"!!!, -
(In-form of sent drones!) -
To turn all of their mighty yachts -

INTO tiny dingy boats!!!,

FOR((YOU SEE!!))...

BETWEEN - Pledges - BETWEEN - Praises - BETWEEN - The Unwavering Resolve - BETWEEN - The Ukrainians - BETWEEN - Heated Exchanges - BETWEEN - Neighbors & Strangers - BETWEEN - Waters of Perils - BETWEEN - Snakes & Sailors - BETWEEN - Certain Death - BETWEEN - Love of Country - BETWEEN - All hands on deck! - BETWEEN - Recommendations - BETWEEN - The telling of a Russian warship, To: "GO FUCK YOURSELF!!!" - BETWEEN - Lines of Communications - BETWEEN - NATO - BETWEEN - EU - BETWEEN - 50 Cal. Gun Barrels - BETWEEN - 5 Dead Russian Generals - BETWEEN - The Polish Air Force flying Russian MiGs,...

(((THE STAKES HAVE REACHED THE NEW HEIGHTS OF ITS LIMITS!!!)))

And(((AS SUCH!!!)))...

BETWEEN - G20 - BETWEEN - G7 Summits,...

(((THIS IS NOT THE TIME!!!)))

FOR...

Stutterings - BETWEEN - Stammerings - BETWEEN - Hemmings - BETWEEN - Hawings - BETWEEN - Mumblings!!!,

AS...

The NEED to have - HAVE been HAD -
(By a needy group!) - NEEDING TO -
HAVE the Summits -
TO suppress - The pressing -
OF nuclear buttons!,

AS...

(Emotions and egos ARE flexed!)

FROM...

((Their OWN buttons BEING pressed!!))

FROM...

(((THE PRESS applying pressure - TO - their buttons BEING pressed!!!)))

(((OY VEY!!!)))

AS...

Headlining every Daily Times Herald,...

AND...

(((THAT THERETO - OF - THEE IMPENDING PERIL!!!))),...

ARE the ramifications,...
OF China's understandings of sanctions,
(((At the brink,..Of WWIII!!!))) -
IF x FOR: Thee "Making of Arraignments" -
IF x FOR: Thee "Abetting and Aiding" -
(((OF WHICH - UPON WHICH - AND - DEPENDENT UPON!!!))) -
OF thee persistence - OF thee insistence -
NOT TO provide Russia's military - ANY assistance!!!, -

And...

(((SPEAKING OF assistance!!!))))...

AS...

(Citizens worldwide)...(ARE making sacrifices!),...

As(FOR!)...

(OUR money)...(WE'RE running through!),...

As(WITH!)...

(THESE - Through-The-Roof-They-Must-Be-Out-Of-Their-Minds - GAS PRICES!!)

AND SOOOOOO...

(((CAN WE GET SOME ASSISTANCE?!?)))

'CAUSE...

(((IT'S NOW LONG OVERDUE!!!)))

'CAUSE...

(BEFORE long!)...

(((The days of the harkenback - WILL BE right back - BEFORE long!!!)))

(((OF WHICH - SPEAKING OF)))...

AS...

(((WE harkenback)))...

((To the Days of Presidents Nixon & Carter - AND - The OPEC Oil Embargo!!!))

AS...

(FOR WHEN YOUR daddy's gas prices overnight BECAME a thing of the past!)

AS...

(FOR WHEN YOUR gas tank's drops were on its last!)...

AS...

(((FOR WHEN YOU WERE IN NEED OF SOME GAS!!!)))...

(Oh, Sure!)...

(YOU could go to Shell - Sunoco - Mobil - Texaco - BP - Hess - And/Or - Esso!)...

AS...

(((FOR WHEN the gas lines were SOOOOOO long and SOOOOOO slow!!!)))...

AS...

(TO THE FRONT OF THE LINE)...(YOU HAVE FINAAALLY GOTTEN TO!)...

AS...

(FOR WHEN IN LINE YOU WERE IN FOR AT LEAST AN HOUR!)...((OR TWO!!))

As...

(The gas station's attendants present have discovered)...

That...

(Today is an "odd" day)

AND...

((YOU HAVE AN "EVEN" NUMBER!!))...

AS...

((THE LAST DIGIT ON YOUR CAR'S LICENSE PLATE!!))

(Oh, brother!)

AND...

(((OY VEY!!!)))

AS...

(((FOR YOU NO GAS GETS PUMPED IN THAT CAR OF YOURS TODAY!!!)))

But...(Psst!)...(HEY, READER!)...(I digress)...

'CAUSE...

(Please believe!)

AND...

((NOT allegedly!!))

FOR...

(JUST AS WITH EASE for me),...

TO RHYME - The Ukrainian Capital City of "Kyiv" -
WITH: The Ukrainian City of "Lviv",
((BOTH OF WHICH - ARE UNDER SIEGE!!)),
((BOTH OF WHICH - INCLUDING - THE CITIZENS AND RESIDENTS)),...
ARE: (((FINDING IT HARD TO BREATHE!!!))),...
FROM: AND - OF - AND - AS IF -
(((BEING PLACED-ALL-UP-IN AIRPLANE OVERHEAD COMPARTMENTS!!!))),

AS...

Kyiv and Lviv,...
ARE: BEING "Compartmentalized",...
BY: ((WAR CRIMES - AND - OVERHEAD BOMBARDMENTS!!)),

AS...

The citizens and residents,...
THOUGH - ((FAR FROM AFFECTIONATE!!)),...
DO AS: THEIR OCCUPYING-INHABITANTS!!,...

AS...

(THEY TOO compartmentalize!!),...

AS...

(THEY decide - TO - finally dry THEIR eyes!!),...

FROM: AND - OF -
THEIR Homeland's destruction! -
And: THAT TOO - OF - THEIR homes!!,
(Locked ALL-UP-IN a compartment case),...
WITH: A classic case of Stockholm Syndrome!,

(((OY VEY!!!)))

And so...(Psst!)...(HEY, READER!)...(I guess I just get goin' I guess;)

'Cause...

(The "teachings" above - WAS - the "setting-up-of"),...

TO RHYME - "Digress",...
WITH: Thee alleged use - OF - "Bombs of Phospherous"!,

Though...

(((LEST WE FORGET!!!)))

It's ONLY fake news -

Dependant upon -
IF you have the freedom -
Of which side YOU BELIEVE to choose!,

And so...

(((BACK TO, OUR: "BRAVE SOULS SHOW"!!!)))

AS(((WE)))...

Gotta avoid bullet holes,
Gotta avoid running -
Outta camera rolls,
(Gotta go digital!),
Gotta avoid those bombs,
Thee creators -
Of all of those -
Craterous holes!,

All While(And ALL THE WHILE)...

Gotta avoid capture,
Gotta avoid my soul,
Being lifted -
Clear-up -
To the sky -
Like the rapture!,
(And yet - capture!),

For(You See)...

Once I find the right,
Moment in-frame,
(IF I get lucky!),
I'll have the time -
To do more than just to -

"Raise n' Aim"!,

For(YOU See!)...

To capture the day -
Thru the night -
TO STAY alive -
Is a brave soul's job -
We're brave souls,
Avoiding bullet holes,
SO MUCH MORE -
THAN "Raise n' Aim"!,
So much more than a job,
(And you find THAT out right-quick -
ONCE the heads start getting lopped!),

For(YOU SEE)...

From the sea -
To the inner city -
From the deserts -
To the outskirts -
Brave souls,
Are down in the thick of it all,
Down in the Aires that are Buenos -
All the way up to the Himalayas!, -

Brave souls,
Are more than adventurers,
But don't call us courageous,
(YOU CAN'T contain us!),
THIS path IS contagious!,
With a photographic eye,
That's the way God made us!,

For(You See)...

If it's heinous?,
There ain't NO hiatus!,
Can you blame us??,
MOST brave souls are nameless!,

AND SO...

Brave souls,
WE GO!!!,
To the massacre in Vegas,
(Gotta make the shutter click!),
Once got a tip on a precinct,
That: THAT'S WHERE the flames is!,

SO...

(Please don't place shame on us shamus!)

FOR(YOU SEE!!)...

Brave souls,
GOTTA GO!!!,
Capture the pics the most-efficacious,
That'll make us the most-famous!!!,

AND SO...

(((NO MATTER HOW HARD I TRY!!!))),...

I find that every time I close my eyes,
To begin the counting of white sheep,...
All there is - I do it seems -
Is in the end I end up with,...
THE COUNTING OF WHITE Z's!!!,...

(((OY VEY!!!)))

AS...

(My photographic eye)...(FINDS its way back to its viewfinder!),...

AS...

(For me)...(there will be NO sleep!),...

AS...

(I begin)...(yet ANOTHER night!),...

OF...

(The counting of)...(((WHITE Z's!!!))),...

OF WHICH - IN MY viewfinder - I'M AFTER to capture! -
OF WHICH - (((SHOCKED x SHELLS))) = (((PTSD))),
OF WHICH - UPON ME - SLEEP has so decreed,...
TONIGHT: YOU WON'T BE CAPTURING (((ANY ZZZZZZ's!!!))),...

(((OY VEY!!!)))

AND SO...

(SINCE upon me to doze)...(IS looking LIKE a no-go!),...

Under the cover of night,...
To arrive,...
(As soon as the lighting is right!),...
I make the treacherous trek,...

(((BACK TO THAT JUNGLE GYM AND SWING SET!!!))),...

For(You See)...

With the right gust to blow,...
Away all that black smoke,

Or perhaps even those helicopter blades -
Will be enough to clear some of,...
(((That thick black smoke away!!!))),...

SO...

THAT: "The Message" -
(I'M after TO capture!) -
SHALL: BE accurately conveyed!,

FOR((YOU SEE!!))...

This pic of mine -
The most-efficacious -
WILL be sure to make its way -
Onto ALL the front pages,
(Just inside of the doors!!) -
OF every gas station -
(AND in OF) -
ALL the corner stores!! -
In stacks -
Where the newspapers are stagged -
IN the right light,
IN the right f-stop,
Right IN their tracks,
EVERY exiting customer WILL stop!!,
(THEY'LL ALL be in a gaze!!) -
Staring at the front page!! -
((THEY WON'T BE ABLE TO TURN AWAY!!)),
((THEY WON'T EVEN BE ABLE TO TURN THE PAGE!!)),
OF the playground most-twisted,
OF my pic the most-efficacious!!,

ALTHOUGH...

(((FIRST AND FOREMOST!!!)))...

Gotta avoid bullet holes,
Gotta avoid running -
Outta camera rolls,
(Gotta go digital!),
Gotta avoid those bombs,
Thee creators -
Of all of those -
Craterous holes!,

All While(And ALL THE WHILE)...

Gotta avoid capture,
Gotta avoid my soul,
Being lifted -
Clear-up -
To the sky -
Like the rapture!,
(And yet - capture!),

For(You See)...

Once I find the right,
Moment in-frame,
(IF I get lucky!),
I'll have the time -
To do more than just to -
"Raise n' Aim"!,

For(YOU See!)...

To capture the day -
Thru the night -
TO STAY alive -

Is a brave soul's job -
We're brave souls,
Avoiding bullet holes,
SO MUCH MORE -
THAN "Raise n' Aim"!,
So much more than a job,
(And you find THAT out right-quick -
ONCE the machetes begin giving "armless village" chops!),...

For(YOU SEE)...

From the sea -
To the inner city -
From the deserts -
To the outskirts -
Brave souls,
Are down in the thick of it all,
Down in the Aires that are Buenos -
All the way up to the Himalayas!, -

Brave souls,
Are more than adventurers,
But don't call us courageous,
(YOU CAN'T contain us!),
THIS path IS contagious!,
With a photographic eye,
That's the way God made us!,

For(You See)...

If it's heinous?,
There ain't NO hiatus!,
Can you blame us??,
MOST brave souls are nameless!,

AND SO...

Brave souls,
WE GO!!!,
To the massacre in Vegas,
(Gotta make the shutter click!),
Once got a tip on a precinct,
That: THAT'S WHERE the flames is!,

SO...

(Please don't place shame on us shamus!)

FOR(YOU SEE!!)...

Brave souls,
GOTTA GO!!!,
Capture the pics the most-efficacious,
That'll make us the most-famous!!!,

For(You See)...

THERE'S A WAR IN UKRAINE!!!

AND(Herein lies),...

WHY: The jungle gyms AND the swing sets,...
WILL NEVER look the same!!!,...

2.5 million thus far made tracks to Poland,
(((SOME of them - EVEN - made tracks BACK!!!))),
TO: Help fight the war!,
AND: To the resistance support!,...

Buuuuuut...

NOT if YOU are African!,
(OH NO NO NO!!! - NOT FOR THE AFRICANS!!!)))),

They WEREN'T ALLOWED - On THOSE tracks!,
They WEREN'T ALLOWED - On THOSE trains!,

And...

(((EVERY DAY - ALL DAY - ALL OVER CNN))),...

The Resistance STILL haven't -
Received the weapons they've requested! -
(The Ukraines are STILL waiting on them!!),
The weapons STILL haven't made it in!!!,
((((AND the sky is STILL open!!!!)))),...

And...

(((ONE DAY - NOT: "One day..." - RATHER - FOR: "ONE DAY")))...

Casually making its way,...
Onto the Mass-Media-Airwaves,
For one segment,
(For NO MORE than a few seconds!),
Were the Africans that felt betrayed -
(AND ALL BECAUSE they were African!) -
AND because they ARE African,...
THEY WEREN'T ALLOWED ON THOSE TRAINS!!!,

AND...

(((IT AIN'T HAVE SHIT TO DO WITH N95 MASK MANDATES!!!)))

'CAUSE...

During thee mass exodus,...

(((ALL THAT SHIT JUST SEEMED)))...((TO))...(Go)...away...

FOR...

THERE AIN'T NOTHING LIKE A WAR,...

TO: DISTRACT DETRACTORS - AS - WELL AS - DISTRACT THE MASSES - REGARDLESS - OF WHAT YOUR RELIGION, AGE, RACE, OR SEX IS - OR IF - YOU'RE A DEMOCRAT - BE YOU - A REPUBLICAN - AN INDEPENDENT THINKER - OR - A CONSERVER OF OPINION - WHETHER - YOU ARE - A SLEEPWALKER WALKING ON EGG SHELLS - OR - ARE "WOKE" - OR - ARE "PRO MASK" - THAT: HAD A TICKLE-OF-A-COUGH - EVEN SO - THERE WAS NOTHING FUNNY ABOUT THE WAY YOU FELT - YET - REFRAINED - AND - REMAINED - "ANTI-VAX" - MADE TO: STAND SIX-FEET BACK - MADE TO: PUT BACK ON OUR MASKS - MADE TO: BACK-AND-FORTH - FROM - LATEST-BREAKING-LIVE-NEWS-BROADCAST - TO - LATEST-BREAKING-LIVE-NEWS-BROADCAST - FLIP - FORTH-AND-BACK - MADE TO: BRIDGE THE GENERATION GAP - AND - ZOOOOOOM - GET-UP-TO-SPEED - 'CAUSE - MOST OF US NEVER HEARD OF THAT! - MADE TO: GO BACK TO SCHOOL AFTER HOME SCHOOL CAME BACK - MADE TO: PUT BACK THE TOILET ROLL PACK - OF - THE QUOTA - YOU WERE OVER - MADE TO: FEEL<LESS<THAN<AND<TAKEN<ABACK - WHEN - THEY LABELED YOU NONESSENTIAL - LIKE - WHAT THE FUCK IS UP WITH THAT??? - AND - HERE ARE THE COLD-HARD-FACTS: A LOT OF THE "NONESSENTIAL DOORS" - OF - THE "MOM N' POP'S" - OF WHICH - WERE CLOSED AND LOCKED WITH FORCE - NEVER MADE IT BACK!!!

'CAUSE...

(ONCE MASSES' MONEY ARE MADE OFF THE BACKS OF THE MASSES?),..

(Psst!)...(((HEY, READER!!!)))...(guess what?)...

(((WE ARE ALL MADE SLAVES!!!)))

FOR...

THERE AIN'T NOTHING LIKE A WAR,...

TO: (((DIVERT THE MASSES))) x (((DIVERSIONARY TACTICS!!!))),...

AS...

TO: (((WHAT'S REALLY GOING ON???))) x (((DURING THESE DAYS!!!)))

(((OY VEY!!!)))

AND SO...

(WHEN this war IS over!)...

FOR...

(((THAT TRAIN-STATION-BULLSHIT!!!)))

And(For)...

(How that story just came and went),...

(Psst!)...((HEY, READER!!))...(((I have A THOUGHT FOR YOU!!!)))...

Hmm...

(((Wouldn't THIS BE SOME shit???)))

(Of the Africans - THAT - WERE MADE to stay!),...

IT'LL be THEIR kids,

ON the swing sets!,
AND playing ON the jungle gyms!,
Once upon a time,...
Where once whence upon,
The kids of the Ukraine played!,

(Psst!)...((HEY, READER!!))...(((I TRIED to tell YOU!!!)))...

(((Those jungle gyms and swing sets - WOULD NEVER - Look the same!!!)))

FOR((YOU SEE!!))...

(((THE<Africans<were<valued < LESS<THAN >
The>price>of>the>seats!!!)))

And...

During these days,...

(((THE DAMN-SHAMEFUL PART!!!)))

In the year 2022,...

(((THAT SHIT LOOKED MORE LIKE DURING THE DAYS OF ROSA PARKS!!!)))

And...

(Oh, Sure!)

Reparations were made!,

TO: The VICTIMS -
OF: “The Ukraine-Train-Seat-Trade”! -
BY WAY - (((OF: AN EXTENDED STAY IN WAR-TORN UKRAINE!!!))),

FOR...

(Of sorts!)

It's the reverse slave trade!,

(Oy vey!)

But...

(THIS time!)

TO FIT the benefit,...
Africans DIDN'T make the trip!,

'CAUSE...

(THIS time!)

They WERE MADE to stay!,

FOR...

(((WOULDN'T THIS BE SOMETHING?!?))),...

IF AT THE END OF THIS WAR,...
All-up-in the maternity wards,
"The Africans of Ukraine" ARE being born!,

FOR(YOU SEE!!)...

Inadvertently,
Certainly,
(It appears to me!),
(CURRENTLY!!!))),...
The Russians WON'T be -
The ONLY ONES expanding THEIR shores!,

FOR...

(((AFRICA TOO HAS NOW EXPANDED INTO EUROPE!!!)))

(Psst!)...(((HEY, READER!!!)))...

I guess we'll just call it a "Casually of War".

WHITE SHEETS IN A BOX

The weak cardboard box's wear,
Shows its age,
But does very well,
Concealing the contents true intentions,

As true as the age,
Of the intentions,
Of the contents,
Worn by its concealer,

Though, truly concealing,
The weak,
Because, the contents intentions,
Truly shown.

YOUR WAY

"If your goal,
Is to bullshit your way,
Throughout your whole life,
Throughout your bullshit life,
Will be a hole." - RHW

INCENDIARY FEATHERS

master-manipulators,
master-embellishers,
frauds,
thieves,
bums,
and your vanishers,
con (wo)men,
compulsive-liars,
deadbeats,
ethically-deceasers,
and hearts of Freeze Dried Folgers,
No bridge to high,
Burnt on both sides,
Learn to fly,
Throw yourselves over.

POSSESSIONS

"A fool has but two possessions. Pride and Denial.
And lacks two others. Accountability and Shame." - RHW

WHEN APROPOS MET JUXTAPOSE, I SUPPOSE

Apropos...

A fool has but one choice.

Juxtapose...

Accountability or Pride.

Apropos...

A fool WILL choose Pride,
OVER Accountability!

Juxtapose...

A fool's Pride WILL BE,
THEIR only and final possession.

Apropos...

A fool WITH Pride AND NO Accountability,
Will NOT only NOT have Accountability,
The fool will NOT have Shame,...additionally!,

Juxtapose...

And, THEREFORE, will NOT have Pride AT ALL!!!

Apropos...

Can one HAVE Pride?

Juxtapose...

If one DOES NOT have Shame??

I suppose...

(ONLY a fool WOULD think so;)

TOO PRIDEFUL FOOL

The Devil, IS a "fooler"!

And so...

The Devil, IS a ***FOOL!!!***

Taken many forms,
DON'T be fooled BY these fools,
Which tends to be the norm,

Only a fool full of foolish pride,
Will fully fail to take accountability,
For a fool will place the blame on thee,
For a fool don't feel a fool when they lie,

As...

The fool continues...

To take kind hearts and TRUE ARTISTS,
And TRUE businessmen and women,
DOWN to their pre-planned fool-ass destination!,

The place with empty pockets,
AND nonsense!,
AND discards them!!,
(Read and heed thee alarm, friends!!!),

A shitty-fool...

Shittin' all over REAL PEOPLE,
REAL PEOPLE,...
THAT ARE REALLY ABOUT SOMETHING!!!,

And...

THAT kills a shitty-fool!

'CAUSE...

A shitty-fool knows they AIN'T really ABOUT nothing!

REAL PEOPLE,...
THAT HAVE BEEN really fooled!,
And ALL they REALLY JUST TRIED to do!,
WAS to work with A fool!,
TO HELP a fool!,
JUST TO BE FOOLED!!!,

As...

THE REAL ONES,
BEEN GRINDIN' HARDER,
THAN the fool, FOR the fool,
WHICH makes a fool,
In their FOOLISH head,
FEEL as though they are smarter!,

FOR...

The fools,
ARE full of themselves!,
THEY'LL LET YOU do ALL the work!!,
They'll LET YOU burn up ALL YOUR money!!!,

KNOWING...

The ARE ill-equipped!,

KNOWING...

The ARE just full of shit!,

KNOWING...

That THEY AIN'T shit!,

KNOWING...

They were NEVER about it!,...the fool with foolish pride.

Well,...Have YOU?!?

Hmm...

(Have you ever felt embarrassed)...(FOR someone?!?)...

THOUGH...

(NOT FROM)...

Someone having tried,
To make a bagel,
Out of a toasted bun!,

RATHER...

With each bite - seemingly increasingly,
In the corner of their mouth - (((DISGUSTINGLY!!!))),
(((Unbeknownst OF THE growth!!!)))...
OF toasted-crumbs & creamcheese!!,

(NOR FROM FOR)...

On a HOT summer's day,
Behind someone you walk - (((NOT stalking!))),

RATHER...

It's just 'cause - Down the sidewalk,
Y'all JUST HAPPEN - TO BE headed the same way!,

Well...

(Maybe it's MORE than that!)...

AS...

(YOU try to hold in YOUR laugh!)...

AS...

(YOU'VE been watching from blocks back!)...

(((THE loooooong-stringy-stretchy-pink-snapback!!!)))

FROM...

THAT someone,
HAVING STEPPED ON,
A piece of bubblegum!,

(NOR FROM FOR)...

Half a roll of toilet paper,
BEHIND someone dragging,
Clear ACROSS the floor!,

FROM...

THAT SOMEONE having,
Just stepped out,...

FROM...

A public restroom door!,

(NOR FROM FOR)...

Milk passing from laughing,
Back up past the tonsils,
Shooting out through someone's nostrils!!,

Nope.

RATHER...

WHEN SOMEONE,
OUTTA' SHEAR JELOUSY,

FEELS THE NEED,
To play YOU LIKE,...
YOU are dumb!,

So...

I'LL just relax,
Observe AND put distance,
Between - THE NERVE - of that attack!,
(WON'T EVEN call them out ON that attack!),

'CAUSE...

(((I ALREADY know!))),
THEE EMBARRASSMENT,
I'M feeling - FOR THEM,
FOR THEM - (((TO feel it???))),
(In, of, and FOR themselves!),
I KNOW - They ALREADY lack!!!,

For(YOU SEE)...

(((TRUST & BELIEVE)))

I AIN'T worried 'bout being shunned!

'CAUSE...

I KNOW - between - the two??,
There's only - ONE - foolish one!

YUP

"Never waste your time in an attempt to inform,
a shitty-person of just how shitty they are.
Shitty-people know that they are shitty.
And they're more than cool with that." - RHW

4x400

Loyalty and Brotherhood: Only go but so far.

Money: Gets snatched like a baton.

One's Word: Is only as good as its source.

NOW...

((((Pay CLOSE ATTENTION to the rest of **THIS** report!!!!))))...

AND...

(Do YOURSELF a favor!)...

AND...

(Hear WHAT I say!)...

'CAUSE...

(In **THIS** race?)...

IT'S...

Pussy: THAT'S running the anchor leg!

DEFINITION OF A FRIEND

Friend(s) (def.): ("Humans"), People, that, have hidden (and, their OWN) agenda(s), that, gather (exclusively) together, more frequent than not, (and/or) remain in contact with one another (frequently, or not), solely (AND, FOR, THE SOLE PURPOSE OF), to keep up WITH their hidden (and, OWN) agenda(s!), (a.k.a. layin' the "groundwork") with, (AND, FOR), ("Humans"), people, that, they FEEL, as though, DON'T have (their OWN) hidden agenda(s!), (AND/OR), THAT, WON'T/WOULDN'T (won't/wouldn't "implement") do them (AS) dirty, (WITH, their OWN hidden agenda(s!)), equal to (and/or), (MORE SO), THAN, THEY WOULD DO (and/or), PLAN TO DO, WITH, THEIR (OWN) hidden agenda(s!), WHICH (IS WHY!) THEY, gather (exclusively) together with, (more frequently), THAN not, (and/or) remain in contact (constant, dependant upon, the severity, (AND/OR) the cruelty OF THE "dirtiness", OF their OWN, hidden agenda(s!)), in so, (AND FOR), and, in that, this "friend" CAN (better THEIR odds!), OF "Deployment/Activation", in so, (AND, FOR), AND, IN THAT, this "friend" CAN "increase" THEIR ODDS, (of THEIR OWN "Success Rate") OF fooling "their friend(s)", with, (AND, FOR), their OWN hidden agenda(s!), WHILE (AND, ALL THE WHILE), leading (and, MAKING) their "friend" TO BELIEVE (AND FEEL!) AS THOUGH, (THAT), you're a "friend" (AND, a "friend" OF their's!) AND, THAT, "YOU'RE CRAZY" ('CAUSE),...they wouldn't do such a thing to you (a "friend").

(For the definitions of "Bro" or "Fam", read this shit again!).

CARVED IN STONE
WITH AN EDGED WEAPON-DAMAGED VERTEBRAE BONE

“You’ll never find me standing in the new friend line.” - RHW

NAH

"Just because they're your peeps.
That don't make them my peeps." - RHW

DEFINITION OF SYKE

Sacrificed **Y**our **K**ind **E**nergy

IT ALL COMES DOWN TO FUCK YOUR FEELINGS

It all comes down to "fuck your feelings".

(And this explaination may have you reeling!)...

If a motherfucker is on some "other shit",
(You know,...BEING slick AND ignorant!!),
AND they're so **BOLD** while committing it,...

But...

TO YOU,
You consider them TO BE a friend!,
(OR,...at the very least,...aquaintances!),

SO...

You question yourself - AS TO HOW - you're viewing it!

AND SO...

To "call them out" on it,...YOU'RE hesitant!!!

But...

(I want ALL Y'ALL to remember this)...(YOU go right ahead AND call them out on it!)

'CAUSE...

It's quite apparent,...
THEY DON'T GIVE A FUCK about YOUR feelings!!!,
((YOUR judgement's NOT errant!!)),

'CAUSE...

((The so-called "slick" ARE the MOST transparent!!))

(Psst)...(Hey, Reader!)...

DON'T YOU WAIT!!!,
DON'T YOU DARE HESITATE!!!,

'Cause(THEE kick in the balls!!)...

(((IF you DON'T call them out on it???)))...

(Psst!)...(Hey, Reader!)...(Guess WHAT Y'ALL???)...

YOU'LL FEEL LIKE SHIT!!!!!!,
(And they'll SEE that shit!),...

AAAAAAND...

STILL THEY WON'T give a FUCK HOW YOU FEEL!!!,
(I'M TALKING NOT EVEN a lil' bit!),

SOOOOOO...

(DON'T YOU DARE WORRY 'BOUT)...

OF: HOW they MAY FEEL?,
OR: OF HOW it MAY sound??,
(It's really quite simple),...
STAND. YOUR. GROUND.

For(You See)...

THEY DON'T GIVE A FUCK ABOUT YOUR FEELINGS!!!,
THEY DON'T GIVE A FUCK HOW YOU'RE FEELING!!!,
AND SINCE THEY DON'T GIVE A FUCK ABOUT YOUR FEELINGS???,
YOU BEST GIVE A FUCK ABOUT YOUR FEELINGS!!!,
GET THE FUCK UP OUT YOUR FEELINGS!!!,
(Don't make NO sense for both y'all to be feeling bad;)
YOU'LL GET SUCH A GOOD FEELING,

GOING RIGHT AT THEIR FEELINGS!!!,

(Psst)...(Hey, Reader)...(From ME, to YOU!)...

(((SEND THEM REELING!!!)))

'Cause...

It really all comes down to,...
"FUCK YOUR FEELINGS!!!"

LAST LAUGH

It's not about having the last laugh.
It's about not giving a fuck,
About being the one,
Having the laugh last!,

About being the one?
NEVER give a fuck!

'Cause...(guess what?)...

NO ONE gives a fuck!!!

THE OTHER SHOE

"The sound the other shoe makes when it drops,
is the sound of the S.W.A.T. Team at your door." - RHW

STRIPPERS AND COPS

Strippers and Cops,
Strippers and Cops,
All the fun starts and stops,
With Strippers and Cops.

TWISTED

People wonder why I wear my beard twisted?,
It's 'cause I strive to be like no one,
I succeed at being different!,

People wonder why my beard is twisted?,
It's 'cause I ain't never scared - I ain't trying to hide,
My identity is never hidden!,

People wonder why I wear my beard twisted?,
It's so I can't be falsely accused and identified,
For doing something that I didn't!,

People wonder why my beard is twisted?,
It's 'cause if I ever do - do some shit,
I want those to know who I did it to - to know the fuck who did it!,

People wonder why I wear my beard twisted?,
It's 'cause people stay bitin' my shit - and stay never givin' me credit for it,
But y'all can't bite the beard twist - without me gettin' credit for it!,

People wonder why my beard is twisted?,
(It's 'cause of one of the greatest things I've ever heard),...
A young father saw me - then told his young kid,
"Son, when I grow up? I'm gonna dress and look like him!".

REFRIGERATOR DOOR

You know you're high,
When you think to yourself,...
"Why is the refrigerator door,
Closing in slow motion??,
But everything else,
Is moving at normal speed!",

And...(fiiiiinally!)...

AT the conclusion,
Of the closing,
Of the door,...

You see that your dog,
Has been sitting there,
Thee entiiiiiire time,
On the kitchen floor!,...

AAAAAAAND...

Your doggy got a look in his eyes,
Having been staring at you,
((Thee entiiiiiire time!!)),...

AAAAAAAND...

Those eyes are like:
"THAT HASH got YOU forgetful!,
You selfish bastard!,
YOU ate up ALL the cake!,
NOW reach up in that cabinet,
And GET US BOTH some pretzels!!"

THE ENABLER

Is the enabler the enabler,
because they love the enabled?,
Or is it because,
the enabler loves the enabled,
more than the enabled love themselves?,

Do the enambled enable the enablers to enable the enabled,
because the enabled have more love for the drugs,
than the enabled have love for the enablers?,
Or are the enabled actually the enablers,
by giving kind hearts attacks of manipulation and guilt?,

So incessant are the enabled,
enabling the enabler to enable the enabled.,
While all along,
in actuality,
they're enabling themselves.,

The enabled flip scripts like they're directing movies.,
But to put the blame on themselves?,
Well, now, that would be some flip script shit!,

Why is it then,
the script gets flipped like a stolen prescription pad,
by placing blame on the enabler,
when the enabled are enablers themselves?,

Is the enabler the enabled?,
Because it certainly would appear,
that the enabler suffers as much if not more,
than the enabled.,
So in essence,
they are one in the same.

TYPES OF KINDS

There's two types of people in the world.
The kind that plunder.
And the kind that rooted,
For the Road Runner.

There's two types of people in the world.
Me?
I'm the kind that always wanted the Coyote,
TO kill that fucking bird!

NIGHT BIRDS

Those night birds,
Early had to learn,
Those night birds,
For the early morn,
Do so now yern,
Those night birds,
For early they have learned,
Those night birds,
TO BE the early-fucking-birds!,
Those night birds,
DO SO set themselves up first,
Those night birds,
AS to NOT be taken of their turn!

THE CROW

Lest we forget,...
Lest we fail to even consider or realize,...
When it comes to the eagle?,
The crow, already knows,...
It can't soar as high!,

BUT(YET!)...

(It takes the fight TO the eagle!)

Staying engaged,
IN that fight,
With the eagle,
IS the crow,...

UNTIL...

(No longer physically ABLE do so!)

For(YOU SEE)...

The crow,
Is instinctually willing TO fight,
A much larger and superior opponent,...

The crow,
Does so,
'Til no longer ABLE to fight!,

(Seems a lil' foolish)...(DON'T IT??)

For...

The crow,
STAYS in the fight,

Til' the point of death,

(((OR 'til DEATH itself!!!)))

And so...

Does the crow,
Have foolish pride???,
(I say, "No!"),

And(SINCE)...

Crows CAN count!,
They SHOULD know better!,
Than to go after an eagle,
With a seven-foot wingspan!!,
((SURELY they can count ALL those feathers!!)),

(Psst!)...(Hey, Reader!)...

(Don't ever think the crow isn't smart!)

FOR(YOU SEE!!)...

(What the crow HAS)...

Is heart.

(NEVER underestimate the power of the heart!).

SMELL THE ROSES

I stop to smell the roses.

But...

In a different way...(In my own way)...

And so...(Psst!)...(Hey, Reader!)...

For YOU,
(((FOR ALL OF YOU!!!))),
To YOU,
THIS is what,
I have to say!,...

YOU ever see,
In the spring,
A large bird being,
Chased by,
Two smaller birds,
In the sky???,

(I'M sure THAT YOU have!)

AND(SINCE)...

(SPRING is coming back!!!)...

THIS spring...

I WANT FOR YOU,
((TO MAKE SURE YOU DO!!)),
TAKE notice TO that!,

'CAUSE...

The two smaller,

Out of "THEIR" territory,
Are chasing the LARGER!!,

'CAUSE...

The nest,
Of the two smaller,
The larger - WILL raid,
And EAT their eggs!!,

AND SO...

In the spring,
WHEN YOU SEE,
THAT happening,
I WANT YOU to look off TO THE SIDE,
(('Cause,...WHEN YOU DO??)),
YOU'LL SEE an even smaller bird,
((Just battin' his lil' wings!!)),
AS fast as he can,
TO come join the fight!!,

AND(THE THING IS)...

The smallest of the birds?

Well...

He just MADE the fight HIS biz!

'Cause...

The larger bird probably,
WASN'T EVEN ANYWHERE NEAR,
The smallest bird's nest!,

FOR(YOU SEE!!)...

The LARGEST bird had NO plan,
TO land,
TO raid,
TO commit,
AN egg robbery!!!,

But...

(That lil' bird)...(peeped a fight happenin'!)

AND...

(((RIGHT THEN AND THERE!!!)))
HE decided,
To join THAT fight,
IN flight!!!,

AND...

That lil' bird,
((Is just battin' his lil' wings!!)),
AS hard AS he can!!,

(Psst!)...(HEY, READER!)...

(Remember when I told YOU to LOOK OFF TO THE SIDE???)...

'CAUSE...

(WHEN YOU do!)...

YOU'LL SEE that far more smallest,
((he'll be EVEN smaller THAN THE OTHER TWO!!)),
Flyin' from waaaaaaay out in the distance,
((He can't get there fast enough!!)),
TO join the fight AND ADD some assistance!!,

(psst)...(hey, reader)...

(The one that's goin' as hard as he can - head first - into a headwind?)...

That's me.
Always has been.
And always will be.

(((I LOVE WATCHIN' THAT SHIT!!!)))

So...

Yeah.
I stop to smell the roses.
All the time.
Just in my own way.

NUTSHELL

"What's me in a nutshell?,
I'll beat your ass,
For trying to put me,
In a nutshell.
That's me in a nutshell." - RHW

THE ART OF COOL

"NEVER SWEAT the insignificance." - RHW

BEING FINE 101

Don't like me?,
I'll be fine.

Never liked me?,
I'll be fine.

Just now not liking me?,
I'll be fine.

Used to like me,
And now don't like me?,
I'll be fine.

Like me, but used to hate me,
But just now, you're gonna hate me again!?!,
I'll be fine.

Bought into the bullshit,
And don't even know why?,
I'll be fine.

For((YOU SEE!!))...

I just grind,
Mind mine,
And climb my own crest,

Hmm...

(I guess,...I'M JUST ONE FINE MOTHERFUCKER, I guess;)

THE COMPANY YOU KEEP

"At this point,
Depression is like an old friend,
Returning to say hello,
And keep me company." - RHW

MY THREE AMIGOS!!!

"Just like alcohol and addiction,
Suicide is always there waiting for me.
MY THREE AMIGOS!!!
I am NEVER alone." - RHW

DEATH MUTE

"The little voice in my head committed suicide." - RHW

MAKE IT BLOODY, WITH A 'CIDE OF NOTATION

First of all...

Fuck each and every last one of y'all!

Nah...(Not really:)

But...(**MOST** of y'all;)

"CHAMBERS,...PARTY OF ONE!"

What comes around,...goes around!

THE DIFFERENCE

(Psst!)...(HEY, READER!!!)...

If you knew exactly,
One minute from now,
YOU were going to suffer,
A massive heart attack,...

Would YOU dial 911?

Or...

Just sit there,
And take the pain?

Then...

You ain't me.

MAN OF MARBLE

"Everything I've been through,
I needed to be through." - RHW

BRUSH UP ON LIFE

"Is it art that imitates life?
Or life that imitates art?
Doesn't matter.
Live both." - RHW

ANIMAL LOVER

"I don't write about puppy dogs and double rainbows,
'cause I don't want those double rainbows, one at a time,
to strangle the shit outta all those puppy dogs, two at a time." - RHW

MYGRAINE

“My writings aren’t-so-much in-yer-face so-as-more-so a-kick-in-the-head.” - RHW

CHRISTMAS MORNING

"I believe God puts people in our lives for a reason.
And, I too, believe, He too -
removes people from our lives for a reason.
And, with that thought in mind -
I believe God gives us all gifts.
And, then He, leaves it up to us -
to recognize what those gifts are.
So that we can then follow our own paths." - RHW

YOU'RE WELCOME

I believe,
My belief,
In Eternal Damnation,
Led me to believe,
In my belief,
That's why y'all are still living.

THE ART OF DEPRESSION

(Psst!)...(Hey, Reader!)...

I want YOU to take a look into YOUR mind...

And...(((Right ABOUT this time!!!)))...

At the edge of a once-sundrenched-farmer's-field,
Still standing tall - YET - yeilding to gravity's field,
(((Using YOUR MIND'S POWER!!!))),...
YOU WILL BEGIN TO SEE all those rows,
(((OF DEAD SUNFLOWERS!!!))),...
FOR ROWS AND ROWS AND ROWS!!!,...

And...

ALL WILL have thier dead sunflower heads,
DROOPED forward - AND hangin' low!! -

And...

ALL WILL be brown, gray, brittle and stark,
(((for, as far, as, YOUR MIND'S EYE goes!!!))),...

And...

WHAT YOU WILL SEE,
(((is what!!!))),
I ALREADY KNOW!,...

AND(THAT'S)...

ALL THESE DEAD SUNFLOWERS,
NECKS WILL BE BOWED,
AND FROM THEIR DEAD SUNFLOWER HEAD'S WEIGHT -
ALL THESE DEAD SUNFLOWERS,

DON'T STAND UP SO STRAIGHT - ANY MO',
AND ALL THESE DEAD SUNFLOWERS,
LOOK DOWN AND DEPRESSED,
(with their dead sunflower heads hangin' low:(

And so...

(((WITH ALL CERTAINTY!!!)))...

I WANT YOU to focus on,
This ONE dead sunflower,
Mat'r fact - The shortest ONE,
(((IN PARTICULARLY!!!))),

(Psst)...(HEY, READER!!!)...

You see - THIS ONE??,
(((THIS ONE - RIGHT HERE!!))),
YOU SEE - HOW THIS ONE,
Is leaning forward MORE,
THAN ALL the rest??,

(Psst!)...(Hey, Reader!)...

Take a look around in YOUR MIND...

(DON'T give me THAT SHIT!)...(((I'm SERIOUS!!!)))

I WANT YOU to SERIOUSLY,
Take a look at ALL of these,
DEAD SUNFLOWERS (((WITH me!!!))),

And...(ON this I do not jest;)

(Psst!)...(HEY, READER!)...

Check it, ...Ok. NOW,...ARE YOU ready, FOR this?!?...

IT'S LIKE THEY'RE ON A MARCH!!!,
YOU SEE that FORWARD "body lean"???,
(((FOR ROWS AND ROWS AND ROWS!!!))),
POSSESSED BY ALL OF THESE!!!,

(They ALL have a slight "body lean" to them!)

AND...

(THEY'RE ALL leaning in the SAME direction!)

One by one. Out in that field. They stand on their own.

(((FOR ROWS AND ROWS AS FAR AS YOUR MIND'S EYE GOES!!!)))...

THOUGH...

TOGETHER they're all tilted forward,
(((IT'S LIKE THEY'RE ALL ON THE SAME MISSION!!!))),
Marching TOGETHER in solidarity,
IN THEIR VERY OWN funeral procession!,
They LOOK LIKE AN ARMY,
MARCHING TOWARDS death!!,

BUT...

They're ALREADY dead!
(And THEY know it!)

For(You See)...

They stand tall on their own,...together,...
One by one.
When they're fully alive in the sun!,

BUT...

When they know IT'S TIME to die?,...together,...
One by one.
They all lower their heads!,

And...together,...
One by one.
Lean towards death!,

(psst)...(hey, reader)...

BUT(YOU SEE)...

It's not until THE LAST sunflower,
HAS dropped its head,...

(THAT it LOOKS like they're ALL taking that march!),...together,...

They wait,...
They wait UNTIL,...
THEY WAIT UNTIL THE LAST ONE,...

HAS dropped its head IN death,
(Is the flower of the sun),...

And(then?)...

IN death.

(((THEY ALL march TOWARDS DEATH!!!))),...together,...

(Psst!)...(HEY, READER!)...

NOW...

(((IN YOUR MIND'S EYE)))...Look at THAT ONE IN PARTICULAR...

YOU SEE HOW IN YOUR MIND'S OCULAR,
The head is heavier and FULLER,

Of THIS ONE? - THAN all the others?? - IN PARTICULAR???,

FOR(YOU SEE!!)...

When THIS ONE IN PARTICULAR FINALLY decided,
To bow its head and die,...

Well...

The stalk like a stake in the ground couldn't take it!,
(((It HAD TO lean forward MORE than ALL the others LIKE this!!!))),
Causing too much stress on the neck,
Was the HEAD of this SINGULAR,
Set so HEAVY & LOW,...(oh, damn, sorry y'all, here we go!),...
Reminiscent of a SET of TESTICULAR!!,

(OY VEY!!;)

For(You See)...

It looks like,...it looks like,...like,...

It NEVER HAD its head up at all!,

It looks like,...

It probably went through its whole-entire-short-life,
(((JUST LIKE THIS!!!))),...
WITH its head down,
Looking down AT the ground!,

LIKE...

(It COULDN'T WAIT to die:(

THIS ONE IN PARTICULAR,

AIN'T EVEN AS TALL AS all the OTHERS!!,...
(HE NEVER GREW!!!),

It looks like,...it looks like,...like,...

(To get it up - it never had the will to try:(

FOR(YOU SEE!)...

THAT ONE IN PARTICULAR,
ALREADY KNEW - THEY didn't HAVE TO -
Wait ON HIM - For THAT "DEATH MARCH" to begin! -
(OH! NO!! NO!!! NO!!!!),...

(Psst!)...(Hey, Reader!)...

For(You See)...

(((HE'S BEEN WAITIN' ON THEM!!!)))

Now(LOOK HERE!!)...

HIS head is ALL FULL OF SEEDS,
(that died too soon!),

And...

HIS stalk is FULL OF GREEN LEAVES,
(even HIS PETALS STILL look fresh!!),

AND...

HIS head EVEN looks MORE yellow,
(than ALL THE REST!!!),

FOR(YOU SEE!!!)...

Way too early in life,
HE just dropped his head!,

AND...

(((GAVE-THE-FUCK-UP!!!)))

(Psst!)...(Hey, Reader!)...

(((TELL ME,...tell me, YOU SEE THAT,...right?!?)))

‘CAUSE...

THAT’S - The: “Art of Depression”.

MY LIFE

It went fast.

GIVE ME

Give me days of the Space Trolley,
And tree forts in a tree,
Give me days of backyard football,
And, "Here I come!", after, "One, two, three!",

Give me days of Park & Rec.,
And walking to the farm,
Give me days of thinking the world is good,
And never knowing harm,

Give me days of Tonka Trucks,
And playing in the dirt,
Give me days of the sounds of cicadas,
And never knowing hurt,

Give me days of racing bikes,
Around the neighborhood,
Give me days of kickball,
And everything happening exactly as it should,

Give me days of little league football,
And little league everything,
Give me days of dreaming about summer,
Even though it's only turning spring,

Give me days of Halloween,
And yelling, "Trick or Treat!",
Give me days of going somewhere,
By walking on your feet,

Give me days of snowball fights,
And playing with toy guns,

Give me days of crab apples,
Bees and the hot sun,

Give me days of softball,
Eating dinner, then back on the run,
Give me back those days,
Because they were a lot of fun.

LIFE

"One's life is like the only snow-covered car on the road. You wonder where it went and where it's going?" - RHW

GREAT BALLS OF FOCUS

It takes balls to dare to be great.

BUT...

It takes hard work and focus,
TO BE great!

STRUCK DOWN

"Who people think they need in their lives,
to be a star, is their star." - RHW

EACH AND EVERY TIME

Rejection used to hurt me.

NOW…

It does me a favor!

SAVVY?
(NOT a question!)...RATHER...(Can YOU REALLY feel this?)

"Believe what you're supposed to understand." - RHW

BROWN-HEADED COWBIRD

"More than less,
More or less,

One thing,
I know,

I know,
I know,

One thing,
About more things,

Than...

More things about,
One thing,

More or less,
More than less. - RHW

PREEMPTIVE-PRESUMPTION > PRESUMPTUOUS-PRETENTIOUS- -PRESUMPTIONS

When you LET a snake believe it possesses,
The hands it lacks to possess,

The knife,
In your hand's possession,

Your destiny will to be,
Face down in the grass,

In the same grass...

That your blood will ensure,
Will never be shorter,

The same blood...

Bleeding heavily,
Out your back.

THOUGHT VS EXPECTATION

Thinking you'll be let down.
Knowing you'll be let down.

CONSUMPTION OF CAKE

If I had my druthers, (WHICH I do!),
I'd stick to my laurels, (WHICH I am!).

READ BETWEEN THE BATTLELINES

“I don’t write to offend.
I write,
to offer.
I don’t write to appease.
I write,
to push.” - RHW

RHW

Well-thought-of, or, well, thought of.

I WANT THIS ON MY TOMBSTONE

1967 - FREE

RECEPTIVE TO FORCED PERSPECTIVE

"Having a kid, helps you keep things in perspective, when perspective, is the last thing you want." - RHW

I WILL

I have piece of mind.
I have strength.
I have goals.
I have power.
I have the power of God.

I am special.
I will succeed.
I will win.
I will survive.
I will.

I, FLED.

I fled,
To a higher state of consciousness,
I fled,
Now I'm constellation's mist,
I fled,
Duckin' suckas - they don't exsist,
I fled,
From a state of worthlessness,
I, fled.

www.ingramcontent.com/pod-product-compliance
Lightning Source LLC
Chambersburg PA
CBHW060848120626
46553CB00001B/17

* 9 7 9 8 9 8 5 6 6 0 1 4 2 *